Diversion Books
A Division of Diversion Publishing Corp.
443 Park Avenue South, Suite 1004
New York, New York 10016
www.DiversionBooks.com

For more information, email info@diversionbooks.com

First Diversion Books edition January 2014

Print ISBN: 978-1-62681-241-3
eBook ISBN: 978-1-62681-237-6

NO LABELS:
A SHARED VISION FOR
A STRONGER AMERICA

EDITED BY **GOVERNOR JON HUNTSMAN**
FOREWORD BY **SENATOR JOE MANCHIN**

DIVERSIONBOOKS

CONTENTS

Thank you for reading *No Labels: A Shared Vision for a Stronger America*. In the pages ahead, you'll find a portrait of a new governing process. It's a call to change the way Washington does business—and finally break through the gridlock that's become all too familiar.

We aren't going to answer every question in this book—but that's because this is just the beginning of a new conversation. In future books, we'll offer even more details about our problem solving approach, our next steps, and how you can get involved in creating a national strategic agenda for American success.

Ultimately, you're going to help shape what comes next. Your work will help write these next books. And it's up to you to determine what the story ahead is going to be.

This is the beginning of a historic movement—and we're thrilled to have you along for the journey.

Thank you,
No Labels

FOREWORD
THE POLITICS OF PROBLEM SOLVING

BY SENATOR JOE MANCHIN

I'll always remember the first time Jon Huntsman and I discussed the potential value of No Labels. At the time, I was the newest member of the United States Senate, and Jon had recently returned from serving as our country's ambassador in China. We knew each other pretty well from our days as governors— elected and reelected the same years—and even though we were from different parties, we'd spent serious time talking about everything from education to tax reform, from jobs programs to our shared love of motorcycles.

Together, we thought we'd seen just about everything—but we'd never seen anything like No Labels before. And when we first talked about this new organization dedicated to a politics of problem solving, we both said the exact same thing: *Finally*.

Ever since I'd gotten to Washington, I'd been feeling more and more discouraged by the politics of division and point scoring I saw playing out in our nation's capital. Nothing could have been more different from the way I had chosen to govern West Virginia. In Washington, I met too many people who thought that the other side wasn't worth talking to, period. I saw the way that members of both parties spent hours every day in meetings focused on fundraising, winning elections, or destroying the opposing party. With all that, there wasn't much time left to actually govern.

I knew it didn't have to be like this. In fact, I'd seen firsthand the way governing can actually work. When I was a governor, I wasn't able to just ignore the other party or citizens of differing opinions—and I never wanted to. I had budgets to pass and governments to run—and I had to work across the aisle to get it done.

In West Virginia, we had a distinctly American approach of problem solving, finding realistic solutions, placing country first, and governing with the next generation in mind. That was always our core motivation, even if some of us had differing party affiliations. That's why I was so excited when I heard about No Labels. *Finally*, I thought, *someone is pushing for that same commonsense approach in Washington.*

I knew it could work—and I was excited about the possibilities. So the first chance I got, I started meeting with Americans from all over the country who wanted to be part of this movement. They intuitively knew that this represented something different—something that actually spoke to the vast majority of Americans. The more I got involved, the more optimistic I got about this effort's potential. Early last year, I jumped at the chance to sign on as a national leader of the No Labels movement—right alongside my friend Jon Huntsman.

You'll hear a lot more about No Labels in the pages ahead. But simply put, No Labels stands for something vitally important—and utterly commonsense. It stands for the basic principle that if we want to move forward as a country, we need leaders who are willing to sit down with anyone—conservative, liberal, or anyone in between—so long as they are willing to work to achieve shared success for America.

We need our leaders to recognize that having principled political beliefs doesn't require an all-or-nothing approach to governance.

And we need leaders with humility—who recognize that maybe you don't always have all the answers and that the people on the other side aren't somehow evil or stupid by default.

These are the values No Labels stands for. In the chapters ahead, you'll read about our campaign to put these values into action—and bring about the change so many Americans know this country is capable of—the change this country deserves.

Politicians always tell us that we need to unite our nation—but no one ever actually tells us *how* they plan to do it. That's why this book—and this new campaign—is so different. In the pages ahead, you'll read about the "how." It starts with getting leaders to build consensus around shared national goals—and yes, they do exist—and then figuring out solutions to meet them together.

No one is ever going to get everything they want with this approach. But that's rarely a realistic possibility, anyway. Instead, this process will offer a way to forge agreement about where we need to go as a nation *before* the negotiations start raging. This way, both sides can collaborate—each giving or taking where needed—until they can reach their mutual objective. They can find a way to move forward together—instead of being driven apart by every small political battle of the day.

This is an actionable approach toward real progress—and a realistic way forward for America. Because ultimately, we are all on the same team. We are all Americans. It's time for us to come together to do what needs to be done. That's what No Labels is all about—and I'm proud to be a part of it.

INTRODUCTION
SHARED VISION, COMMON GOALS: A BETTER GOVERNING PROCESS

BY GOVERNOR JON HUNTSMAN

Which country represents the greatest danger to the United States?

That was the question the Pew Research Center asked more than a thousand Americans last November. Participants weren't given a list of options; they were just asked to name their choice. The top of the list wasn't particularly surprising; in a world of nuclear threats and economic warfare, Iran and China were obvious choices. But the next country named was more of a shock. According to the American people, the third country on the list of America's greatest enemies was America itself.

How did we get here? How did we get to a place where the American people have concluded that we are literally one of our own worst enemies?

Maybe it was when our leaders in Washington turned running our government into an exercise in chaos and uncertainty, flailing from one late-night crisis to another, closing last minute deals, or shutting down the government when they failed to reach an agreement. Maybe it was when the president's sweeping health care law passed without a single Republican vote. Or maybe it was when Republicans responded by resorting to unprecedented, even dangerous, tactics to try to roll it back.

When the American people look to Washington, they see a city divided. Two parties who don't meet together, eat together, or even seem to like each other. Two sides that never even *try* to work together. Different teams who never lay out a common agenda to strengthen our country. Instead, there are two separate visions and two separate agendas—with a constant war of attack ads, vitriol, and all-around drama standing between them.

The more Americans hear about what's happening in Washington, the more convinced they become that our best days are behind us. And it's hard to blame them. But luckily, even though Washington is filled with America's representatives, its dysfunction does not represent America. And if you look at America as a whole, there are a lot more reasons to feel optimistic.

Yes, we have big challenges to face as a country. In the last fifteen years, we went from a balanced budget to record, unsustainable deficits. We still promise our children that Social Security and Medicare will be there for them, but we don't take the steps to guarantee that. Meanwhile, we're still climbing back from a recession that cost us millions of jobs, shrank our economy, and shattered our sense of economic security. We know that harnessing a new energy economy could create countless jobs and unleash amazing economic growth—but we still don't have a clear energy policy to take advantage of the opportunity.

The challenges are real. No one disputes that. But these challenges are also solvable. Not in theory, or in the abstract. The solutions are out there—and it's not too late for our leaders to come together and pass them into law.

It might surprise you to hear that despite all the noise and rancor coming out of Washington, there are still plenty of people on both sides of the aisle who *want* to solve problems. From the staunchest conservatives to the most committed liberals, our elected leaders care deeply about this country. And for the most part, they're more discouraged than anyone that our two parties just can't seem to get to "yes" anymore.

So what's the problem? Bold systemic reform ideas like getting money out of politics or putting an end to congressional gerrymandering are certainly worthy and important endeavors—but they are tough, multi-year, state-by state slogs. Ideas like that may never come to fruition—or come in time. Because the simple fact is that we need a better governing system that takes advantages of the best impulses in Washington, not the worst. And we need it *today*.

The good news is that we can start changing the system right away. Common ground in Washington really *does* exist if only our leaders are empowered to find it. Our leaders really can be problem solvers again—they just need a governing process that brings them together instead of pulling them apart.

At No Labels, we've seen a vision of how our government can work. We are a citizen's movement of Democrats, Republicans, and Independents dedicated to a new politics of problem solving. Our membership includes members of Congress from both sides of the aisle, academics, business leaders, and hundreds of thousands of citizens from every corner of our country. They don't agree on everything, but they definitely agree that we need our leaders to stop fighting and start working together again.

This is exactly what the American people are calling for. We asked them in a poll late last year, and *ninety-seven percent* of Americans said it was important that our next president be a problem solver. These days, it's impossible to get ninety-seven percent of Americans to agree on the toppings for a free pizza, or much of anything else—but in this case, they were nearly unanimous. We *need* our leaders to be problem solvers once again—and all of us know it.

In this book, we build on No Labels' work to create a national constituency for problem solving to offer a path forward toward changing American politics. In the pages ahead, you'll hear from leaders from every part of American life—from business, government, economics, and academia. You'll hear from Problem Solver members of Congress who still want to work across the aisle and get things done.

These contributors come from different places and backgrounds, but they lend their perspectives and their voices to this book because they all believe that we need to do better as a country. We need to actually know where we're going—and we need to work together to get there.

In the pages ahead, we'll tell you about our campaign to change American politics. It's a campaign to end a governing process that simply drifts between divisive debates, political posturing, and outright crises. Instead, we want to replace all that with a problem- solving process. And that starts with forging a new strategic agenda for our country.

Think about the State of the Union. It's a moment when a president is supposed to gauge where we stand as a country—and where we need to go. But these days, no matter which party holds the Oval Office, these addresses are mainly just laundry lists detailing the agenda of one party. The president announces priorities, and then the other side jumps up in protest. Before long, we're mired in gridlock—and neither side ever achieves much of anything at all.

If we had a national strategic agenda, this could all be different. The president and the leader of the opposition could meet before the State of the Union to agree on what goals we can pursue over the next year. It would shift the focus to setting shared goals—and the entire process would be recast. Now, the two sides would get agreement on goals *before* the policy-making process starts. And instead of constantly getting jammed up in gridlock, both sides would have a shared end to work toward once the negotiations start.

With this publication, No Labels is charting this new way forward. We're beginning the work to establish a new process of governing in our country—starting with a national strategic agenda.

Like every initiative No Labels has proposed, this agenda will be a product of discussion and agreement from every part of the political spectrum. It will require leaders to come together to explore the shared goals we need as a nation. In the pages that follow, we suggest some places they should start—with goals that most Americans, whatever their politics, whatever their labels, believe are vital to the well-being and growth of our country. But ultimately, this process will require our leaders to come together to determine what's possible, and what we can still achieve together.

If we can to forge agreement on a national agenda—based on mutually agreed upon objectives—we can finally start to break the gridlock in our politics today. That's a path forward that both parties should rally around. Because we just can't keep going muddling along like we are now. It's time to start solving problems again. It's time to get down to work. It's time to stop fighting and start fixing.

STOP FIGHTING, START FIXING: THE NO LABELS STORY

BY NO LABELS

I believe that we can change politics in America for a simple reason: I've already seen No Labels' incredible progress toward bringing our leaders together. Today, No Labels hosts the only organized forum in Washington for members of different parties in Congress to come together, talk openly about the challenges we face, and discuss the whole range of possible solutions. The ideological spectrum represented in that room is as vast as our country itself—but when folks sit down at that table, they're ready to solve problems together. In this chapter, the No Labels co-founders tell the story of how it all began— and what's coming next.

—Jon

The No Labels co-founders were as anxious and jittery as candidates on an election night as they made their way to Alfred J. Lerner Hall on the cold New York morning of December 13, 2010.

Driven by a firm belief that our political system was badly broken—and an instinct that much of America shared their frustration—the veteran political advisers and elected officials had spent the previous year laying the groundwork for a new organization that would push back against the culture of extreme partisanship and acrimony that was gripping Washington. These Democrats and Republicans, some of the most experienced and respected political minds in America, had traveled the country—

to libraries, college campuses, living rooms, and coffee shops—
to plant the seeds for a new movement among citizens of all
political stripes.

Now the day of the official launch had finally arrived. The
founding leaders had set an audacious goal: to get one thousand
people from all fifty states to come to New York—on their
own dime!—for the kickoff of No Labels, a new grassroots
organization that would put problem solving and the good of
the country ahead of partisan politics.

They'd lined up an impressive array of speakers and panels
(even a Broadway star to sing the national anthem), purchased
box lunches for the expected crowd, and invited reporters to
cover the day-long event.

But as the No Labels founders made their way to Columbia
University on that raw December morning, they held their breath.

They had built the organization. Would the people
actually come?

HOW TO BUILD A NETWORK FOR PROBLEM SOLVING

It had been easy for No Labels co-founder Nancy Jacobson,
an adviser and fundraiser for major Democratic Senate and
presidential candidates for nearly three decades, to find fellow
political professionals who were as disenchanted with the
breakdown in Washington as she was and eager to find a way to
build bridges across the partisan divide.

For years, the gulf between the two parties had been
growing, with partisan poison preventing action on the urgent
issues of the day, from the budget to the environment, often
bringing the government to a complete halt. The election of
President Obama had offered real promise for a new day of
cooperation and unity. But by 2010 that hope had vanished when
the Affordable Care Act passed without a single Republican
vote, and the flames of vitriol and hyperpartisanship raged
hotter than ever. Special interest groups fanned those partisan
fires, promoting divisions and rewarding bad behavior.

Outside Washington, the Tea Party was staking out terrain

on the conservative side, Moveon.org on the progressive side. In the vast space occupied by those who wanted their elected officials to work together and get things done—most Americans—there was nothing.

Jacobson found a kindred spirit on the other side of the aisle in Mark McKinnon, a leading Republican strategist who had worked for President George W. Bush and Senator John McCain, and had for years seen the optimistic, reformist hopes of well-meaning politicians crumble in the harsh partisan light of Washington. He too believed there was a hearty appetite throughout the country for better behavior among elected officials—for real collaboration and problem solving.

Jacobson and McKinnon reached out to their respective networks, and soon a long list of like-minded political veterans and presidential advisers were in: Bill Galston, a former deputy domestic policy adviser to President Clinton who had long embraced a politics of consensus building; journalist and author John Avlon, who'd been chief speechwriter for former New York mayor Rudy Giuliani; Clarine Nardi Riddle, a former Connecticut attorney general and chief of staff to Sen. Joe Lieberman; former House Republicans Tom Davis of Virginia and Mickey Edwards of Oklahoma; longtime Democratic strategist Kiki McLean; former Kentucky state treasurer Jonathan Miller; former Atlanta City Council president Lisa Borders; and David Walker, U.S. comptroller general under Presidents Clinton and Bush.

The mission also attracted civic-minded business leaders such as Panera Bread founder Ron Shaich and Loews Corp. co-chairman Andrew Tisch. They joined the cause—and the No Labels movement was off and running.

Over several months, these and other thought leaders crafted the vision for No Labels, drawing up a blueprint for a new political infrastructure that would promote problem solving. The gridlock had become so perilous that the founders wanted an action- and results-oriented agenda. They wanted to have immediate impact, so they would leave the systemic changes requiring long-term solutions—such as campaign finance, redistricting, and electoral reforms—to other groups already grappling with such issues. Instead, they would seek rule and process changes—immediate fixes to the system that were palatable to both parties, would bring about real change, lower the ideological temperature, and could be achieved right away.

No Labels would respect the two-party system, embracing the most devoted Democrats and the most stalwart Republicans, the most ardent conservatives and the most passionate liberals. Everyone would have a place at the table, as long as they were committed to putting their country first and working in good faith with the other side.

Finally, the founders made one last decision that became a hallmark of the organization. Though No Labels would be based in Washington—in the early days, a one-bedroom apartment so crammed that one workstation was in the bathroom shower—this would be a citizen-driven movement, its energy harnessed from Americans who wanted their elected leaders to do better. Without the voices of the people, politicians in Washington would never pay attention. So throughout 2010, the founders took No Labels on the road, fanning out throughout the country like a primary presidential campaign to drum up support and fine-tune the mission.

FROM KITCHEN TABLES TO NATIONAL MEETINGS: A GRASSROOTS MOVEMENT GROWS

No one had to tell the teacher in Des Moines or the social worker in Little Rock that the system was broken. Everyone knew it. And they were starved for the sort of commonsense approach to tackling the nation's problems that No Labels was all about.

In Minneapolis, Laurence Reszetar, a young lawyer, had become increasingly depressed and apathetic about politics. He'd grown up in a military family that valued politics, and he eventually became an official in the state Democratic–Farmer–Labor Party. But in the last several years, he'd become disenchanted, especially after getting flak for supporting a St.

Paul City Council candidate who wasn't the party favorite. He felt such extreme party allegiance was dominating the system, from the local level to the national level, where it often led to stalemates and inaction. No one swears an oath to their party, he thought, yet politicians act as if they do. Looking down at his two-year-old daughter and newborn son, Reszetar felt he owed it to his children's generation to hit the reset button.

Lifelong Republican Ted Buerger, an Internet entrepreneur in Westchester, NY, was similarly disillusioned by all the fighting and divisiveness that he felt was preventing any real progress. The passage of Obama's health care bill with Democrats alone seemed to him the symbol of everything that was wrong with politics. Members of Congress had told him there was so much rancor in Washington that it was increasingly dangerous for them to be photographed with colleagues from the opposite party. Buerger knew there had to be a better way to govern.

Democrat Wade Garard of Noblesville, Indiana had avoided involvement in politics since he saw nothing but people on the extremes shouting at each other and no support for pragmatic solutions. The Phi Kappa Psi Foundation director thought No Labels could infuse politics with the sort of fellowship that made fraternal organizations so effective and valuable. He became so enthusiastic that his fourteen-year-old son, Mason, started a No Labels club, the first ever, at his high school, recruiting members from both the Young Democrats and Young Republicans clubs at North Central High.

In Dallas, personal stylist Bobbi Schwartz, a self-described Goldwater/Reagan-style Republican, would often call or write her representative in Congress with strongly held views—often frustration—about the direction of the country and inaction in Washington. She never expected any results. As a small business owner, she felt that if people in the private sector performed as poorly as members of Congress, they'd be fired. When she happened upon a discussion of No Labels on C-SPAN in 2010, she was glued to the television—and hooked. She sent out an email to everyone she knew, telling them that finally, there was a way to do something beyond randomly calling your representative. Finally, there was a way to be heard and try to effect change.

People like Reszetar, Buerger, Garard (and his son!), and Schwartz—and eventually about 100 other local leaders—built the network from the ground up, holding meetings around their kitchen tables or at their neighborhood libraries.

Toward the end of 2010, the grassroots buzz about No Labels was reaching elected officials. The newly elected junior senator from West Virginia, the state's former Democratic governor who'd long been committed to problem solving, felt like he'd found a home when he heard about No Labels. Senator Joe Manchin wanted not only to be a part of this new movement, but to lead it.

He made his way to New York for the launch of No Labels, joining other senators, House members, a governor, big city mayors, and other current and former political figures—as well as citizens from all across America.

When the founders looked out to the audience at Columbia's Lerner Hall, they saw a retired police officer from Alaska, a restaurant owner from Louisiana, a physical therapist from New Hampshire, students from Boston College and the University of Texas.

They saw that the citizens had indeed come—more than one thousand of them, in fact, from all fifty states—some with their families, some from halfway across the continent, all with a determination to get the country moving forward again, and all with a belief that their voices could make a difference.

THE NEXT STEP: TURNING IDEAS INTO ACTION

Since that day, the No Labels network has grown to more than half a million citizens, with leaders and organizations in every state calling on their political leaders to work together to solve the nation's problems. Only two people showed up to the first meeting Laurence Reszetar held at the Washburn Library in Minneapolis. But the next time out, he had an audience of fifty, and by September 2013, he filled the Westminster Presbyterian

Church with five hundred people for a No Labels town hall meeting that was broadcast on public radio.

When Senator Manchin looked for a Republican counterpart to lead the organization, he found a politician equally passionate about changing the dynamics of politics: Jon Huntsman, a fellow former governor from Utah. With the Democratic senator and the former Republican governor and presidential candidate at the helm, No Labels has in its three short years taken the concepts of consensus building and problem solving and transformed them from verboten utterances in Washington to words that are now gaining such currency that they will be on the lips of every candidate as we enter a new presidential campaign cycle.

No Labels has proven that, with an infrastructure for cooperation—something as simple as establishing regular meetings for members of both parties in Congress to come together, talk to each other, and build trust—problem solving works.

The group has produced a series of non-ideological initiatives—many of them simple, commonsense rule and process changes to get the system moving—that have garnered support from both parties and gained traction.

One of the first ideas, No Budget No Pay, was a proposal to withhold lawmakers' paychecks if they can't make spending and budget decisions on time. It became so popular that an entire Senate hearing was devoted to the idea. It became a winning campaign agenda item for California Rep. Ami Bera, who unseated a three-term congressman who had opposed the idea. Ultimately, a version of No Budget No Pay, part of No Labels' Make Congress Work! package, was signed into law by President Obama in February 2013.

Two other reform packages followed: Make the Presidency Work!, a prescription for enhancing the power and accountability of the Oval Office occupant, and Make Government Work! , which features nine proposals to reduce government waste and inefficiency. These proposals have been turned into legislation—with support from members of both parties—in both the House and the Senate. They've proven that members of different parties can still come together around legislation built around commonsense problem solving.

As the No Labels leaders and supporters have worked to build support for their agenda, they've attracted more and more allies on Capitol Hill, lawmakers who've been frustrated by their inability to work with colleagues across the aisle. These consensus-minded senators and House members have banded together to form the No Labels Problem Solvers, a coalition now nearly ninety members strong that meets regularly and is committed to putting the best interests of the country ahead of partisan point scoring.

During the 2013 government shutdown, the Problem Solvers met daily, often in the cold, windowless basement of a Tex-Mex restaurant on Capitol Hill, to try to come up with ideas for breaking the deadlock. As Rep. Charlie Dent of Pennsylvania writes about in this volume, the Problem Solvers came up with a plan that became central to the Senate's successful negotiations.

The Congressional Problem Solvers have also begun to connect with state and local officials, helping to build a dynamic No Labels network across the country that is engaging everyone from big city mayors to college students to thought leaders.

With a burgeoning nationwide network, a significant congressional presence, and ideas that have earned notice and praise in newspapers all over the country, including the *New York Times*, *Washington Post* and *Wall Street Journal*, No Labels is now taking its next bold step to call for a national strategic agenda—and a new, better process for governing. If you're reading this book, you're already a part of it.

If ever there was a moment for such a national agenda, and for a movement like No Labels, it is now. The original founders have grown only more convinced over the last several years that the continued discord and dysfunction in Washington threatens progress and prosperity. Out of nothing but sheer dedication to their country, they continue to commit their own time and resources to No Labels, bringing valuable lessons learned from years in the White House, congressional offices, or campaigns to our political landscape today.

Their vision for what could be—and what should be—also attracts legions of young people from all over who want leaders they can be proud of. The young, energetic back-office staff at No Labels is passionate about changing the culture in Washington. And the organization has become a magnet for scores of college interns who come through its doors each year—so far, 270, hailing from forty states and ten countries outside the U.S.—to be a part of this important movement that speaks so clearly to their generation.

But the heartbeat of No Labels is still a fast-growing citizen army that is telling its leaders every day that they need to do better. They need to put their partisan labels aside and put America first. And they need to start today.

NO LABELS VOICES
REP. CHARLIE DENT (R-PA)

Around Washington, it sometimes feels like we're engaged in trench warfare. Too many seek safety and security in their own trenches—especially if their general reelection seems a sure thing—and no one wants to get out and venture into "no man's land."

The government shutdown was a prime example. We were in a situation of terrible division that led to complete dysfunction, with the leaders on both sides unable to reach an agreement. The leadership vacuum provided an opportunity for members like me to step in, try to come up with reasonable solutions, and get to "yes."

Right after the shutdown, Rep. Ron Kind and I came together—a Democrat and a Republican—and forged a very simple proposal to reopen the government: pass a continuing resolution for six months, repeal the medical device tax, and pay for it with a pension-smoothing provision that was largely agreed to by both sides. We were able to get a critical bipartisan mass in the House to back us, and it really caught on. Our common goal was simple: We shared a very strong sense of governance. It was that basic. We all felt that members of Congress have a basic fundamental responsibility to affirmatively govern the nation and fulfill our most basic functions—funding the government and passing a budget.

The leadership, of course, did not embrace this proposal. But to me it really represented the starting point for the negotiations that helped us break the impasse, reopen the government, and make sure the country did not default on its obligations. The fact that we introduced this proposal into the discussion helped us move off the dime—and it became central to the negotiations. Senators Susan Collins and Joe Manchin carried our proposal aggressively in the Senate.

Though there was a lot of leadership opposition to our proposal, there was considerable rank-and-file support. To me, that represents a glimmer of hope as we move forward. There are plenty of members on both sides of the aisle who want to get beyond this trench warfare. It will require members of Congress who are not afraid to step out of their comfort zones and who are prepared to deal with a backlash for participating in a consensus-driven process for the good of the country.

NO LABELS VOICES
REP. PETER WELCH (D-VT)

Before entering Congress, I was the Senate president in the Vermont legislature. We had a big Democratic majority, but the governor at the time, Jim Douglas, was a Republican.

In 2005, the Democrats passed a controversial bill that would have extended health care to many people in Vermont. I wanted to expand access to health care, but Governor Douglas was concerned about controlling health care costs, so he vetoed it.

But we didn't walk away from the table and play the blame game. The governor and I sat down together, and we recognized that Republican concerns about cost and Democratic concerns about access *both* had merit. So we incorporated our mutual and legitimate concerns into a common goal: access to health care delivered in an affordable and sustainable way. The next year, we passed a bipartisan bill that has served Vermonters well.

Progress takes effort. And it requires political engagement and mutual respect to work through a tough process with conflicting priorities, so you can explain to supporters and adversaries that what you are doing will actually advance a shared goal. That's the hard work of legislating in which all legislators should be engaged.

In Congress, I've found similar ways of making progress by emphasizing areas of agreement rather than conflict. For instance, the Republicans generally haven't agreed with Democratic objectives on climate change, and there continues to be a lot of debate about the science of climate change. But I've found that many Republicans are totally in agreement with Democrats about the benefits of energy efficiency—creating jobs and saving money. So I'm working with Republicans like Cory Gardner of Colorado on cutting energy use in federal buildings and with David McKinley of West Virginia on encouraging homeowners to retrofit their homes.

There's immense potential in partnerships with Republicans on practical, commonsense energy efficiency measures. It's a space where people with different points of view can get something done that's good for the country and, just by making progress together, good for Congress.

One of the highest principles all of us claim is a commitment to getting things done for our country. So how do we do that? Like we do in Vermont, let's focus on the things we can agree on, not just the differences between us. It's an old-fashioned way of working together that we must restore in Congress.

HOW TO CHANGE AMERICAN POLITICS: WE CAN MOVE FORWARD IF WE AGREE WHERE TO GO

BY NO LABELS

When you look at Washington today, one thing is overwhelmingly clear: Our governing process just isn't working anymore. Too many politicians don't want to solve problems—and there's no process in place to bring them to the table. In this chapter, the No Labels co-founders diagnose the problem with our governing dynamics today—and they explain what needs to change so we can create a problem-solving government once again.

—Jon

The stadium was packed by ten in the morning. Despite the burning Texas sun and the stifling humidity, forty thousand people jammed into Houston's Rice Stadium on a fateful morning in September 1962. It's not clear how many in the crowd knew that they were there to witness one of the most important speeches of the twentieth century—but by the time President John Fitzgerald Kennedy was done speaking, there was little doubt that our nation had entered the first moment in a new era of American history.

"We choose to go to the moon," the president said. "We choose to go to the moon in this decade and do the other things, not because they are easy, but because they are hard, because that goal will serve to organize and measure the best of our energies and skills, because that challenge is one that we are willing to accept, one we are unwilling to postpone, and one which we intend to win."

At the time, it wasn't fully clear how we planned to achieve this objective. But as President Kennedy said, simply setting the goal was the first critical step toward success. A goal, as he said, "will serve to organize and measure the best of our energies and skills."

Of course, he was right. Within a decade, we had gathered our resources, brought together our best minds, and stood together as a nation as an American flag was planted on the surface of the moon.

We achieved this historic accomplishment because President Kennedy understood how important it was to bring the country together around a shared sense of purpose. He understood that goals dispel passivity and inspire action. They bring seemingly impossible feats just within our grasp. And that's the same reason that we need a new set of shared American goals today.

We know that this might sound like a pie-in-the-sky dream to you. After all, there have been plenty of well-intentioned movements to change politics before—and a lot of them haven't gotten very far. But our campaign is different. We know it's not enough to just offer nice words about civility and bipartisanship. We know there are plenty of people on both sides with strongly held beliefs—and we don't expect to change that.

Instead, our campaign is based around a simple concept: Right now, all of the dynamics in Washington create a constant battle between two sides. More and more, it seems like our leaders are only focused on the short-term pressures of the moment: the next legislative battle, the next election, the next day's headlines.

That's what we need to change. We need to build a governing infrastructure that actually encourages our leaders to solve problems. And we can start that process today.

THE "PROBLEM SOLVING" INFRASTRUCTURE
If you look at the governing process in Washington right now,

you'll see that most of our elected leaders are determined to govern in a zero-sum, "winner-take-all" manner. But with America divided, both sides need to recognize that neither party can just dominate the other or get everything they want. That's not real leadership—and we'll never get anything done that way.

Instead, we need a governing process that starts with a basic recognition: In an era of divided government, we can only move forward if we can agree on where we need to go. That's why we need a mechanism that pushes the different parties to come together around a shared direction for our country.

Even when Washington has been bitterly divided in the past, common goals have helped turn confrontation into agreement. They change the dialogue, shifting the issue from *whether* we should do something to *how* we can do it. With that simple shift, both sides suddenly have a shared basis to evaluate competing proposals and collaborate to make trade-offs between them.

As you'll see in the next chapter, leaders with views as divergent as Bill Clinton, Ronald Reagan, Tip O'Neill, and Newt Gingrich have proven this point. Neither side got everything it wanted in any of these instances, but once party leaders agreed on where they wanted to go, they found a way to get there together.

Or look at what happened in 1919, when a young army officer joined a convoy designed to test whether America's roads would permit the movement of troops and equipment from coast to coast. He wrote a vivid report of his experiences, and he never forgot how slow the trip was, or how many times trucks skidded off poorly maintained surfaces.

Thirty-three years later, this officer, now a military hero, ran for president, denouncing the condition of America's roads and calling for the creation of an interstate highway system. Although he was known as a cautious and conservative man, Dwight Eisenhower said this: "I see an America where a mighty network of highways spreads across our country." After winning the presidency, Eisenhower used the full powers of his presidency to transform this vision into a national goal, telling Congress in 1955, "Our unity as a nation is sustained by free communication of thought and by easy transportation of people and goods." After tough negotiations about transforming this goal into reality, he signed the Highway Act of 1956. Today, that "mighty network" forms the backbone of our nation, and generations of Americans can't even imagine our nation without it.

Today's challenges may be different, but our country's need for shared purposes remains. That's why No Labels is working to identify shared goals so we can formulate a strategic agenda.

The American people know we can't afford to go on the way we've been going. They're demanding a new politics of problem solving—and now is the time to forge it. If we don't, the alternative is continued gridlock, stagnation, and decline. If we want to pass on a strong, prosperous, secure nation to our children, we must change course. And we have no time to waste.

NO LABELS VOICES
REP. LYNN JENKINS (R-KS)

When I first arrived in Washington in 2009, the Democrats controlled the House and the Senate, and President Obama had just been sworn in. Few would have guessed that a freshman Republican congresswoman in the House would have a chance to not only be heard, but get a piece of legislation passed and signed into law by the president that year. However, through sharing a common goal with my colleagues across the aisle, and making the case effectively, I was able to help forge a bipartisan solution to a tragic problem in my district.

The town of Treece in southeast Kansas lies right on the state border. Essentially neighborhoods of the same town, Treece is literally across the street from the town of Picher, Oklahoma. In the early twentieth century, the area was one of the top zinc and lead producers for World War I and World War II. But after the mining companies left in the 1960s, it became one of the most environmentally devastated areas in the whole country with severe land, air, and water pollution. There were huge piles of toxic mining waste, called chat piles, that looked like little mountains and dotted the landscape. There were sinkholes and uncapped mine shafts that would fill with contaminated water, where children would swim and come home with burned red skin from the acid.

The regional EPA office in Oklahoma bought out and shut down Picher, relocating all the families there. But because they were on the other side of an invisible state line, the families living on the Kansas side of the community were left there and spent years fighting through all sorts of bureaucratic red tape.

A Democrat in the state legislature, Doug Gatewood, brought the issue to my attention during my first month in office. I invited EPA officials to go down and see the contamination and destruction with their own eyes. It really was a sight to behold! After a little convincing, we were able to work together, and then, along with my two Republican colleagues in the Senate at the time—Sam Brownback, now the Kansas governor, and current U.S. Senator Pat Roberts—we pushed legislation through the Democratic-controlled House and Senate to relocate sixty-six families who owned homes and about a dozen renters. In 2012, the town of Treece was officially disincorporated and removed from the map.

It may not sound like good news, but without the buyout these families would have been forced to remain stuck in a toxic wasteland. The story of Treece is a great example of how we really can overcome partisan divides in Washington if we work together in a collaborative way toward a common goal. The way to do that is to put people before politics and communicate effectively. Even when Democrats controlled everything in Washington, three Republicans were able to get something done. People at home don't believe that's possible in today's environment. But if we look past the politics and put people first, it is.

NO LABELS VOICES
REP. KURT SCHRADER (D-OR)

I learned several important lessons about coming together around shared goals during my years in the Oregon state legislature.

As the Democratic co-chair of the Ways and Means Committee, which had total control of all the dollars spent, I was a common target. The Republican leader in the state Senate, Ted Ferrioli, was an especially staunch adversary, always doing his best to undermine what I was doing.

Except one time. There'd been talk of starting a four-year veterinary college for Oregon. As the only veterinarian in the legislature in 2001, I was approached about this and was very inclined to try to make it happen even though money was tight. Since Ted represented a huge swath of agricultural Oregon that was very interested in a functioning veterinary school, I reached out to him. Even though we battled all the time on just about everything, he decided he'd work with me. We gave speeches together on the benefits—I would talk about the small animal and equine end; he'd talk about the livestock end of things. As a result of our coalition, we had overwhelming bipartisan support, and the college came to pass.

That partnership helped smooth the way as we moved forward. I had a little more credibility with Ted and, frankly, he had a little more credibility with me. We were able to work on some of the difficult budget issues that came along with a little less rhetoric and a little more cooperation. You start to build that slow but sure credibility that is all too lacking in many legislative bodies, particularly in Washington.

In another case, I helped broker a compromise between animal rights activists and the livestock community over the question of what to do with dogs who were chasing, and in some cases injuring or killing, livestock. Both sides shared the goal of keeping the animals safe, so we came up with a solution to move the dogs to a different non-rural setting rather than put them down, and that agreement became law.

On a bigger stage, finding common objectives that will lead to a national strategy will take a lot of listening and extreme political courage. But if we can start to coalesce around common goals, admittedly at a thirty-thousand-foot level, that's a first step in helping us define what we agree on, not what we disagree on, and find common ground.

WORKING TOGETHER CAN WORK AGAIN: THE CLINTON AND REAGAN EXAMPLES

BY DR. BILL GALSTON
SENIOR FELLOW AT THE BROOKINGS INSTITUTION

When it comes to politics and public policy, Bill Galston is one of America's top experts. He's served in the White House, authored eight books, and been a part of six different presidential campaigns. As a Senior Fellow at the Brookings Institution, he's used his experience to help address some of America's toughest challenges. He's also a No Labels co-founder—and strong proponent of a national strategic agenda. In this chapter, he argues that this approach isn't just an abstract theory. In fact, it's worked many times in the past. Again and again, even when Washington has been bitterly divided, policymakers have still been able to work together to accomplish a common goal.

—Jon

Enduring policy change in the United States comes about in one of two ways. Sometimes one party is so dominant that it can enact its agenda on its own, regardless of what the other party wants. That's what happened during the early years of the New Deal, for instance, and in the first two years of LBJ's Great Society. But moments like these are rare. More typically, one party enjoys a narrow edge over the other rather than a supermajority, and the parties often divide control between the two houses of Congress or between the legislative and executive branches. In such cases, it becomes necessary to build support across party lines before policymakers can achieve lasting progress.

When the parties can agree on goals, the path to agreement on policies becomes smoother. This was true for Ronald Reagan and Tip O'Neill. It was true for Bill Clinton and Newt Gingrich. And it remains true today.

PRESIDENT CLINTON AND SPEAKER GINGRICH

On September 5, 2012, President Bill Clinton stood before the Democratic National Convention in Charlotte, North Carolina. Amid roaring applause, the former president told the crowd, "People ask me all the time how we got four surplus budgets in a row … I always give a one-word answer: Arithmetic."

That's part of the story. Yes, Clinton led the country to its first balanced budget in almost thirty years. But he didn't do it alone. A balanced budget was only possible because the two parties came to agree on that goal and then found a way to reach it together.

This might sound surprising. After all, the Clinton years are often remembered as an unending succession of partisan battles. But in fact, the parties came together more than once to achieve historic agreements—among them, the deal that finally balanced the budget.

For many decades, the Democratic and Republican parties have clashed over levels of taxing and spending, and both parties have displayed ambivalence about balancing the budget when it conflicted with what they regarded as higher priorities. That helps explain why we have so seldom achieved balance.

When Bill Clinton became president, the economy was struggling to emerge from recession, and the budget deficit was large by historical standards. In early 1993, he resolved a debate within his administration by choosing fiscal restraint over expansive public investment, an approach that reduced the deficit without eliminating it.

In the 1994 midterm elections, Newt Gingrich led the Republican Party to a majority in the House for the first time in forty years. The party's Contract With America featured a balanced budget as a prominent goal.

At first, President Clinton and most members of his party balked. The cuts would be too deep, they said. It wasn't possible in such a short time frame. In February 1995, Clinton released a budget that projected annual deficits of nearly $200 billion through 2005.

Just four months later, Clinton reversed course. In a speech from the Oval Office in June 1995, he endorsed the goal of a balanced federal budget and laid out his ideas for reaching it in the way that he believed would best promote the well-being of the people. He insisted that Medicare, Medicaid, and programs to improve education and the environment must be protected from major cuts. "There are fundamental differences between Democrats and Republicans about how to balance the budget," he said. "But this debate must go beyond partisanship. It must be about what's good for America and which approach is more likely to bring prosperity and security to our people over the long run."

With those words, Clinton reframed the conversation in Washington. At that moment, the parties stopped fighting over whether they wanted to balance the budget. Instead, they started debating the best way to get it done.

The period that came next is often remembered for a partisan battle that ended in a government shutdown. But neither party lost sight of the goal of a balanced budget. When Clinton addressed the nation in the midst of the shutdown, he mentioned the importance of balancing the budget more than ten times. For his part Speaker Gingrich repeatedly underscored his party's commitment to balancing the budget. They disagreed over how quickly the budget could be balanced and what needed to be cut—but they never strayed from that goal.

In the end, of course, the government reopened. The next year Congress passed the Balanced Budget Act of 1997, and Clinton gladly signed it into law. With that law in place—and with rapid growth driving the economy—the United States balanced its budget for the first time in decades and did so for four years in a row.

PRESIDENT REAGAN AND SPEAKER O'NEILL

People sometimes say that Ronald Reagan and Tip O'Neill were able to work together because of their famous agreement that politics should stop at six at night. When Reagan called the Speaker, he was known to ask, "Tip, is it after six o'clock?" Then the real conversation would begin.

This cordial relationship was surely important to the successes O'Neill and Reagan shared. But good manners only got them so far. They disagreed on a host of issues ranging from the size of government to foreign policy—and they fought over them. But when they could agree on a goal, they often found a way to get there together.

Take tax reform. They may have disagreed on many of the specific points, but they agreed that America needed a simpler, fairer tax code. Once they had agreed on that goal, it was just a matter of finding a way to get there.

They found that way forward in 1986, when the president and the Speaker built a bipartisan coalition to enact one of the most comprehensive tax reforms in American history. Of course, both sides had to give ground to get there. The Democrats agreed to drop the top tax rate from fifty percent to twenty-eight percent, while Reagan agreed to raise the capital gains tax from twenty percent to twenty-eight percent. The number of tax brackets was reduced. Despite the forces of countless lobbyists, both sides agreed to strike a number of tax deductions that benefited only the rich and the well connected while failing to promote economic growth. In the end, America had a better, fairer, simpler tax code—and the American people were the winners.

The politics surrounding this issue were just as thorny thirty years ago as they are today. The crucial difference was real commitment by leaders on both sides of the partisan divide to achieve this goal together.

In both of these cases, presidents and congressional leaders found ways to work together across party lines. They can do that again today—and they must. Because while we remain stalled, our competitors won't be standing still, and the next generation of Americans will pay the price.

When President Clinton addressed the nation from the Oval Office that crucial day in 1995, he closed by saying,

> "There are those who have suggested that it might actually benefit one side or the other politically if we had gridlock and ended this fiscal year without a budget. But that would be bad for our country, and we have to do everything we can to avoid it. If we'll just do what's best for our children, our future, and our Nation, and forget about who gets the political advantage, we won't go wrong."

That same spirit should guide us today.

OUR STRATEGY FOR A STRONGER AMERICA

BY NO LABELS

If you've read this far, one thing should be clear above all: Our country doesn't move forward by fighting. We move forward when we have a shared sense of where we need to go. As you've already seen, presidents like Dwight D. Eisenhower, John F. Kennedy, Ronald Reagan, and Bill Clinton all proved this in their times. And we should summon that same kind of national aspiration today.

Our challenges today are no larger than those faced by past leaders. Our skills and resources are just as abundant. What we lack today is not the ability; it's the sense of urgency, and largely, the sense that we have a common goal we can achieve together. Today, we need objectives to rally around as a nation. We need to identify our most foundational problems and focus the thrust of our energies and our talents on solving them. In this chapter, No Labels identifies those foundational problems. They list the goals we need to start pursuing today to make our nation much stronger tomorrow.

—Jon

As we were writing this book, we gathered input from experts of every field and every point of view. We asked them all the same questions: What are the most pressing problems our country faces? What are our greatest strengths and most persistent weaknesses? What should the United States be striving toward today?

We also asked the American people the same questions. We conducted a poll where we asked more than a thousand Americans what our government should be focused on right now. The options ranged from implementing congressional term limits by 2020, to landing humans on Mars by 2035, to everything in between. But ultimately, four major concerns rose to the top.

Right now the American people are worried about America's ongoing jobs crisis and anemic economic growth. They worry about Medicare, Social Security, and the strength—and sustainability—of our entitlement system. They worry about our government's deficits and long-term fiscal health. And they're concerned about our energy security and the way our energy policy—or lack of one—positions us to create jobs and compete in the future.

On each of these issues, the experts and the American people agree. These are the big, foundational challenges that we need to confront. They aren't our only national goals—nor should they be. In their poll responses, the American people made it clear that we need to revitalize our infrastructure, support innovation, and do much more to secure our future for the next generation. They said we need to address education and health care—tax reform and poverty. But first, they want us to tackle our most immediate challenges.

This approach makes sense. Because if we solve our biggest, most fundamental challenges today, we'll be in a much stronger position to tackle every other challenge that we face. We would essentially build a runway from which our national ambitions could take flight.

To that end, we're proposing that we as a nation undertake at least four essential goals that require our urgent effort:

1. **Create twenty-five million new jobs over the next ten years.**
2. **Reform Medicare and Social Security so they are secure another seventy-five years.**
3. **Balance the federal budget by 2030.**
4. **Make America energy self-sufficient by 2035.**

Each of these objectives has been on the table, in some way or another, for many years, but very little progress has been made with any of them. It's not because the solutions aren't clear, but because we haven't focused our talents and resources. That's precisely why the process of setting clear goals is so important. It's the only way to start a process that transforms empty rhetoric into decisive action.

It's one thing for politicians to offer vague rhetoric about "fiscal responsibility" or "energy security." It will be entirely different if they sign onto clear goals with clear measures of success and failure. If both sides buy into a set of shared objectives, it will be possible for the American people to judge the progress that their government makes each year. If something isn't working, our leaders will be able to refine their course to get closer to these ends. And most importantly, it will be possible for the voters to hold their leaders accountable if they aren't working together to get our country where they've all agreed it needs to go.

In the pages ahead, we'll take these goals one at a time. We'll offer our thoughts on why they are urgent today, why they will make us stronger tomorrow, and why we should be able to achieve each one. With all of these challenges, the solutions are out there. We just need our political leaders to work together to figure out how to actually get it done.

CREATE TWENTY-FIVE MILLION NEW JOBS OVER THE NEXT TEN YEARS.

When James Truslow Adams coined the phrase "The American Dream" in 1931, the ideas he inspired were truly radical.

He saw America as a land that was different from Europe for one very important, very unique reason. In America, who you are is defined not by the nobility of your blood, but by your commitment to hard work.

"The American Dream," Adams said, "is that dream of a land in which life should be better and richer and fuller for everyone, with opportunity for each according to ability or achievement."

Well, a lot has changed since 1931.

For one thing, a recent Gallup study revealed that people don't want the same things they used to. The desire for money, love, and freedom used to top the lists of aspirations worldwide.

But now, everyone wants the same thing: a good job. And it makes sense, because money, love, and freedom are all connected to having a good job. A job means the ability to support your family. It means the freedom to live as you choose. A job, above all, is the pathway to the American Dream.

Unfortunately, since the most recent recession, a job is also one thing that's become much too hard to come by.

The Great Recession cost our country millions of jobs. Countless Americans watched as loved ones lost their dignity and their ability to support their families. Of the Americans who were able to find work, more than half were forced to settle for lower-paying positions. Today, more than four and one half years after the official end of the Great Recession, fewer Americans are working than when it began in December of 2007. All told, almost eleven million Americans are still out of work.

This is why creating jobs needs to be a top priority for our elected leaders. And that's why we're calling on our leaders to rally around a crucial goal: to create twenty-five million jobs over the next decade.

This isn't a pipe dream—in fact, there's already some cause for optimism. The unemployment rate currently rests at seven percent, lower than it's been since the 2008 financial collapse. Experts expect job growth to continue steadily over the next decade. The manufacturing sector has seen consistent growth, Americans are buying more homes, and CEOs around the country predict more economic expansion throughout 2014.

We're heading in the right direction, but we could still veer off course at any time. Just look at what happened when our leaders shut down the government last October. In the end, those political theatrics cost our country 120,000 jobs.

Instead of this brand of dangerous gridlock, we need a

simple commitment from Washington. No more self-inflicted economic wounds. Instead, leaders from both sides of the aisle need to recommit our country to job creation. That could mean investing in repairing America's infrastructure. It could mean streamlining regulations to help new and small businesses hire. There is no shortage of great ideas. Right now, there's simply a shortage of political commitment to turn those ideas into reality.

Ultimately, most Americans want the same basic things. They want good jobs. They want to go to work every day, provide for their families, and leave their children a better world than the one they found.

Over the next ten years, creating twenty-five million jobs can restore twenty-five million hopes, twenty-five million opportunities, and twenty-five million American dreams. This is a goal we all need to pursue.

REFORM MEDICARE AND SOCIAL SECURITY SO THEY ARE SECURE ANOTHER SEVENTY-FIVE YEARS.

It's 1940.

Social Security was founded four years ago, and Ida May Fuller is the first person to receive Social Security benefits. It's a time when payroll taxes are low, forty-two workers share the cost for every one retiree, and the retirement age is higher than life expectancy.Ida May lives to be a hundred years old, and she counts on Social Security benefits every single month for thirty-five years.

It's 1965.

Congress and the president have come together to create a new program: Medicare. Now, Americans over the age of sixty-five can retire securely and safely, without having to worry that they won't be able to get the medical care that they need.

It's 2013.

People are living longer, depending on Social Security and Medicare more than ever before, even as the benefits shrink. Life expectancy exceeds retirement by eleven years for men and sixteen years for women, and seventy-seven million baby boomers populate the planet. The elderly make up a greater and greater percentage of the United States population, making entitlements even more unstable. In 1944, there were forty-two workers for every retiree. Today, that number has shrunk to three. The system is becoming less sustainable every day—yet Washington doesn't seem ready to act.

It's 2033.

One billion people on the planet are over the age of retirement. For the first time in global history, the number of people over sixty-five exceeds the number of children under the age of five.One out of every five Americans is over the age of sixty-five, and the Social Security trust fund is now insolvent. That means Social Security can only provide seventy-five percent of promised benefits to the people who need it and have earned it. Meanwhile, Medicare became insolvent in 2026.

As more and more Americans expect to live *longer*, the very systems set up to ensure that they live *better* struggle to survive. After years of hard work, too many Americans retire under a shadow of stress. Ida May Fuller becomes a symbol of a broken promise and a failed system.

That's where we're headed if we don't change course and reform these programs soon. There's no reason to wait—we should get this done right away.

As America's population ages, we'll only need Social Security and Medicare more. Today, fewer than half of American households ages fifty-five to sixty-four have saved enough to retire on. Already, the majority of Americans over sixty-five get two-thirds of their income from Social Security. Our country's retirees literally can't afford to lose out on the benefits they paid for.

For the last half century, we've made a sacred promise to our citizens. In exchange for a life of hard work, your secure retirement is guaranteed. But that promise is about to reach its expiration date, unless Washington takes action.

It's not that we don't know what to do. In fact, many experts—in and out of government—have come up with ways to keep these systems secure for generations far into the future. Washington isn't lacking a way, but increasingly, it seems to be lacking the will. Part of that is a function of politics—the fear, on both sides, that their opponents will use the popularity of these programs as a bludgeon against any meaningful steps toward reform. But largely, the failure to act is not rooted in fear; it's rooted in complacency, in the belief that these problems will be solved someday by somebody else. That kind of logic has put this problem off for too long, and now, we are genuinely running out of time.

That's why we're setting a goal: Reform Medicare and Social Security so they are secure another seventy-five years.

Washington has to rid itself of the habit of kicking questions about entitlements down the road. This is a chance to secure these vital programs for generations. It's a chance to ensure that the children being born today can live with a certain promise that they will receive the benefits they earn. Social Security and Medicare are two of the most important programs the U.S. government has ever created; it's time to restore Americans' confidence in these vital parts of American life.

BALANCE THE FEDERAL BUDGET BY 2030.

"This budget marks the end of an era. An end to decades of deficits that have shackled our economy, paralyzed our politics and held our people back."

With those words, President Bill Clinton put a ribbon on a historic moment. It was a gift to the American people: a balanced budget for the first time in thirty years. As Bill Galston discussed in the previous chapter, our leaders in Washington achieved this monumental accomplishment by working together.

In the 1990s, President Clinton and Speaker Gingrich put their differences aside long enough to turn urgent red ink into a triumphant black zero. And hopes were high at the start of the new millennium as the Congressional Budget Office projected more surpluses to come.

But then, things started to take a turn for the worse. Starting in 2002, we began running budget deficits again—and the deficit exploded to over a trillion dollars in the years that followed.

Recently, we've seen a partial—and welcome—reversal of this trend. At the end of the 2013 fiscal year, the federal deficit fell by thirty-seven percent. For the first time since the financial collapse of 2008, the deficit sits below a trillion dollars. Our economy is getting stronger, and our government is spending less.

Still, even as we move in the right direction, we're nowhere near a balanced budget—and it's not at all clear how our leaders plan to get us there. Politicians from both sides of the aisle do plenty of talking about the deficit. They're eager to pelt the American people with dire predictions, and they're more than happy to tell you who to blame for them. But it's time for them to stop simply talking about the budget and get to work balancing it.

Again, there's no undiscovered secret about how to get this done. Economists across the board agree on ways to balance the budget. Ways that are both fiscally responsible and socially accountable. But these options don't matter if we can't get our leaders in Washington in the same room to talk about them.

Balancing the budget by 2030 wouldn't just be the chance for Washington to make history again. It would be the opportunity to revitalize our economy. It would be the possibility to give generations to come a truly worthy gift: not just a balanced budget, but a sustainable future.

MAKE AMERICA ENERGY SELF-SUFFICIENT BY 2035.

What if we told you that right now, America has the chance to create jobs, spur economic growth, protect the environment, *and* strengthen our national security?

It might sound too good to be true—but it's not a fantasy. Just consider these facts:

Right now, the energy sector has the potential to grow much more quickly than almost every other part of the economy. Over the next few years, the domestic oil and gas industries alone are projected to grow over four times faster than the rest of the economy.Citigroup recently estimated that if we can secure an abundant supply of energy here at home, our real GDP could increase by as much as 3.3 percent. That might not sound like much, but it would mean hundreds of billions of dollars added to our GDP—and as many as 3.6 million new jobs.

This kind of growth could transform our economy. It could kick start a whole new wave of job creation, because for every American job created in the oil and natural gas industries, three more jobs are created in other sectors across our economy. So today, the opportunity is clear. We have the chance to revitalize our economy with jobs ranging from hydraulic engineering, to installing solar panels, to developing the next great innovation in renewable energy. Research today could lead to the idea that powers our cars, heats our homes, and changes all of our lives for decades and even centuries to come.

A coherent energy strategy could unlock all this—but first we need to take advantage of this opportunity.

The good news is that we've already started producing a lot more energy at home in recent years. Today, only thirty-five percent of the oil we use is imported—a major improvement over the peak of sixty percent we hit in 2005. But that still leaves us relying on foreign nations for a considerable share of our energy supply. As a result, billions of American dollars are flowing into the coffers of countries that, to put it lightly, haven't exactly been our best friends in the past.

If we want to change America's energy future, then we need decisive leadership and an effective energy policy. We need a policy that taps more into our existing energy supply while spurring the innovation we need to create viable alternative energy sources.

If we don't create a coherent strategy that allows us to satisfy our energy demands at home, we'll always be left looking beyond our borders for help. That would be enormous missed economic opportunity—an unforced error that we just can't afford.

This isn't rocket science. Politicians from both sides of the aisle agree that we need to take greater strides towards energy self-sufficiency. That's why we're proposing a new goal for our nation. We need to make America energy self-sufficient by 2035. And there's no reason that we shouldn't be able to achieve it.

Policy wonks have already outlined the basic requirements needed to make the transition. If our political leaders from both parties can agree to make this a priority, we know we can get it done. This is a straightforward, commonsense, manageable goal—we just need the political will to reach it at last.

THIS CAN BE DONE

To be sure, there's a lot more we need to do as a country. This is far from an exhaustive list of all of the challenges America faces in this century and beyond. But this is just the first step—a set of mutually reinforcing objectives that will push us forward to a stronger future where we can achieve much, much more.

There will be a lot of tough decisions ahead. Accomplishing any of this is. going to require real trade-offs, and no one is going to get everything they want.

In this book, however, we have purposely stopped short of suggesting *which* trade-offs will be needed. That's the mistake that is made too commonly in our political debates. Too often, political actors start parsing the smallest policy disagreements right from the beginning—before they've ever agreed on what they're actually trying to achieve. Before long, they're completely divided—and all because they got wrapped up in the details before they took the time to build consensus around the big picture.

This book is just the first step toward remedying that problem. It's the start of a three-year campaign to change the conversation—and the mindset—in Washington. It might take an election or two before we see the shift—but ultimately, we need our elected leaders to start reorienting our government toward problem solving.

It won't be easy—but real leadership demands that you

reconcile opposing forces and different points of view. That's what we need for the good of our country right now. Because the solutions are out there—and now it's up to our leaders to get together and work out precisely what to do.

Imagine if the idea of problem solving through common objectives becomes part of the next presidential campaign. It could be game changing. What if the next president starts his or her administration with a clear commitment to building consensus around shared goals? What if he or she met with the opposition even before they're sworn in? And on January 20, 2017, the new president could use his or her inaugural address to tell the country that the two parties have met, and this is what we agree we need to achieve. This is how we can make our country stronger.

It may be easy to look at the scope of our problems—and the boldness of these goals—and think, *this can't be done*. But it can be. Washington has come together many times in the past, often when our challenges were more severe and our divisions more stark. We can do it again. We *must* do it again.

NO LABELS VOICES
REP. REID RIBBLE (R-WI)

I often tell folks at home that they really need to be aware of just three numbers: 218, 60, and 1. Those are the votes you need to pass a bill in the House and the Senate and have the president sign. Any idea or goal that won't achieve those three numbers is not really a strategy. It's a fantasy. So our goals have to begin with positions of compromise or achievability.

In business, you're setting goals almost every day that have to be based on what's achievable, because what isn't achievable is a distraction. Throughout my entire professional experience in commercial roofing, we were always moving toward specific and achievable objectives. When those objectives were shared by both management and workers, we ended up with the best results.

At one point in my company, there was a lot of tension around the idea of worker safety. We were imposing some very stringent safety requirements, and the workers were constantly pushing back. They felt a lot of the rules slowed them down and made them less efficient. One day, when we were working on a church in Appleton, Wisconsin, several of my employees decided to go up on the roof before the scaffolding was underneath them. I ended up firing four people that day, not because they had violated some federal regulation, but because they put themselves at risk, the company at risk, and their families at risk. I had to draw a line in the sand. I told them I don't want to have to go to somebody's mother or spouse or children and tell them their family member is not coming home today.

That was a pivotal moment in the life of my company. My workers realized that safety was not just something being forced on them, but something that was in everyone's best interest. After that, they started contributing ideas about safety measures at the job site. They began to participate in the planning. Once we all had the same goal of creating a safer workplace, our efficiency and productivity increased.

If the two political parties could focus on our shared goals for the country, we could improve our own productivity. We're not that far apart on the big issues. Both sides see the national debt and deficit spending in excess of $600 billion a year as systemic threats to our future. Both sides want to find solutions. But the political parties focus on the differences because they're selling those differences in the marketplace. They're not selling the areas of agreement because that doesn't make for a very good political campaign. To fix these big problems, we have to do it together. We have to have positions of agreement where we can get to 218, 60, and 1—and make something better for the American people.

NO LABELS VOICES
FORMER REP. JANE HARMAN (D-CA)
President, Woodrow Wilson International Center for Scholars

These days it's extremely hard to achieve bipartisan consensus, especially on budget issues. But there's a model for how Congress can work together respectfully and productively. You just have to look at the group of forty members of Congress—equal numbers of Democrats and Republicans—who worked on the Penny-Kasich deficit reduction plan in December 1993, my first year in Congress.

This was another time of deep partisan divisions. The controversial Clinton budget of '93 had passed with only Democratic votes. Many people who voted for that budget, which raised revenue and cut spending, ended up losing their seats in the next election, among them Marjorie Margolies (then Marjorie Margolies-Mezvinsky), the Pennsylvania Democrat who cast the deciding "yes" vote as Republicans jeered and shouted, "Bye-bye, Margie!" In my case, I was reelected in 1994 in an absolute squeaker after voting for the Clinton budget.

Later that same year and in that climate, we almost succeeded in passing a mammoth bipartisan budget bill. Forty of us, led by former Democratic congressman Tim Penny of Minnesota and former Republican congressman John Kasich, now governor of Ohio, reached consensus on a plan to cut $100 billion from the federal budget over five years. That may not sound like much now, but twenty years ago, that was real money! We agreed on measures to slow entitlement programs, mainly Medicare, cut discretionary spending by $50 billion, cut about 250,000 civil service slots, and curb military and civilian retirement benefits. All decisions were unanimous.

The full force of the Clinton administration came down on us, as did other influential voices like Colin Powell, who called to try to talk me out of it. But the bill was put up for a vote on the House floor, and we came within six votes of passing it.

The key to consensus within the group was that all of us shared the goal of responsible deficit reduction. We had a shared goal as well as mutual respect for one another and rules that were totally fair and honored. Our views may have been all over the map, but they weren't hardened partisan positions. There were no teams—no D team and R team.

The No Labels call for a national plan built around shared goals is a sort of successor to Penny-Kasich, albeit on a bigger stage and in a tougher time. The paradigm now in Congress is to blame the other side for not solving the problem instead of working with the other side to solve the problem. In 1993 we were able to pull together for a common objective in a partisan climate, and in a process that was completely respectful, productive, and without any friction. And we almost won.

AMERICA'S TEST: A NATIONAL STRATEGY FOR NATIONAL COMPETITIVENESS

BY PROFESSOR MICHAEL E. PORTER
HARVARD BUSINESS SCHOOL

As the head of the Institute for Strategy and Competitiveness at Harvard Business School, Michael Porter is one of America's leading authorities in the study of national competitiveness. He has authored numerous books including Competitive Strategy, Competitive Advantage of Nations, On Competition, *and* Redefining Health Care. *In this chapter, Professor Porter argues that America is no longer poised to be the most competitive nation in the twenty-first century. We need to restore our competitive advantage—and shared national strategy is the best way to do that.*

—Jon

I can't think of a more important priority in America today than defining our shared goals as a nation and having a national strategy to address them.

Most Americans believe that we still have the most competitive economy. Our prosperity is assumed. We think of our nation as the most productive, innovative, and dynamic, and in some respects we are. Because competitiveness is assumed, the vast majority of attention is focused on social issues.

However, the economic prosperity of the U.S. has been faltering. This began decades ago and has accelerated since 2000, well before the recession of 2008. Job generation has slowed down dramatically, wages have stagnated or fallen except for the most educated, and the proportion of Americans working has dropped to a thirty-year low. The average American is struggling. The American Dream is at risk.

Many people believe our current economic difficulties are the result of the great recession, and that stimulus will be a solution, rather than understanding the fundamental structural problems we face. Most Americans, especially those with higher incomes, don't realize how serious the threat to our competitiveness actually is.

A competitive economy is one where companies operating in the U.S. can compete successfully in global markets while maintaining and improving the wages and standard of living of the average worker. This is the only way our economy can create economic opportunity for all Americans.

A competitive economy is also what allows us to address all the other things we care about. If the U.S. is not competitive, America will have trouble meeting all our other goals and aspirations. Our foreign policy, our ability to create fair rules in the international trading system, and our ability to tackle the many social challenges we face will be severely limited if our economy cannot grow, generate good jobs, support rising wages, and expand tax revenues so we can balance the budget. Right now, we're moving in the opposite direction.

Today's debate is not about competitiveness but on how to divide the pie—who should get more and who's getting too much. We're blaming each other, when the real problem is that the pie is shrinking for a large part of our population.

Still, despite the serious structural problems we face, America lacks any strategy to address them. What is a strategy? A strategy is an integrated set of steps to meet an important goal. A strategy for competitiveness would address the most important and pressing challenges facing the U.S. economy— from balancing the budget to improving mid-level skills—as well as the steps needed to take advantage of our most important economic opportunities like our new energy circumstances.

Strategy involves making choices and setting priorities, not trying to please every constituency or tackle every issue. Once you have the strategy, it becomes the framework against which to test every investment, policy, and bill in Congress. The legislation that should be moved quickly through Congress is that which addresses our core strategic agenda.

The United States is unusual in not having a national strategy. As one who works with leaders all around the world, I can tell you that most nations have a strategy. They set explicit economic goals and create an agenda for achieving them. In South Korea, for instance, leaders have been very strategic about the steps required to move the country to a higher level of skill and technology, which is needed to raise the income level in what has been an upper-middle-income country. South Korea is now a highly sophisticated economy with leading global firms such as Samsung, an increasingly efficient business environment, and a growing pool of highly educated people.

Denmark is another example of a country that has gone through a process of national strategic thinking involving its political, business, and labor leaders. Denmark has done well compared to other European countries that have been unwilling or unable to work across stakeholders and move beyond ideologies.

If we look back over the last century, America has set bold agendas as a nation: universal public education, land grant universities, the interstate highway system, a commitment to open competition and strict antitrust, the National Science Foundation, sending a man to the moon, creating the Internet, and others. These bold agendas built critical national economic assets that enabled America to be competitive.

In the early 1980s, when Japan was recognized as a serious challenge, we came together as a nation to do some deep soul-searching about what America needed to do about it. President Reagan appointed a bipartisan Presidential Commission on U.S. Competitiveness, and important progress took place both in government and the private sector.

Today, we face a far greater challenge than the one we faced from Japan. Part of the challenge comes from the fact that many other nations have raised the education and skills of their citizens, reduced corruption and government intervention, and rapidly improved their business environments.

But our real challenge is from within. America has made little progress in a decade on any of the economic policy steps that we know are critical. And now we need to act before it's too late.

I think most Americans are beginning to intuitively understand that we need a plan. But we don't have one. There is a lot of talk, but everyone is talking past each other and not getting anything done. In America, we're not organized or inclined to be very strategic. We tend to approach things issue by issue. No one gets together to say, "Given all our issues, which are the ones we need to focus on now?"

To develop a competitiveness strategy for America, we need to be brutally realistic about our challenges. Yet right now, political speech is incapable of these kinds of assessments. Instead, we lapse into "feel good" rhetoric while each party or interest group sees its pet issues as the only priority.

That needs to change, because the campaign for American competitiveness is the most important campaign that will be run in America during this era in our history. We have to win this campaign. If we don't, there will be more "have nots," more inequality, and the nation will turn against itself.

I'm still optimistic, because America retains crucial and distinctive strengths. With smart and committed leadership, a new strategy for shared prosperity is possible. This possibility starts with having the right ideas. It starts with a new, shared understanding of what we mean by competitiveness, who is affected, what is at stake, where we stand in America, and how we need to move forward. Once the majority understands the shared goal and the strategy, we will see real progress.

For our political leaders, being strategic will require a very different concept for governing. For us citizens, it will require choosing and evaluating our political leaders based on whether they can accomplish the steps necessary for the nation.

I am hopeful that No Labels, with its focus on bipartisan solutions, can help frame the challenge facing America today in a way that our political dialogue has failed to do—and help create a consensus on a national strategy.

NO LABELS VOICES
DEAN GLENN HUBBARD
Dean of Columbia Business School and Former Chairman of the Council of Economic Advisers

In February of 2001, President George W. Bush stood before a joint session of Congress and laid out his vision for the country.

It was a divisive moment in our nation's history. The year before had seen a bitterly contested election followed by an even more contentious recount in Florida. But now that he was in office, President Bush was calling for a major tax overhaul. "To create economic growth and opportunity," he said, "we must put money back into the hands of the people who buy goods and create jobs."

The moment seemed ripe for another all-out partisan battle. Yet despite the ill will remaining from the election on both sides, President Bush's plan ultimately received bipartisan support. Democrats in both houses of Congress got behind the proposal—and Democratic Senator Max Baucus, who later became chairman of the Finance Committee, helped write the tax reform package that Bush ultimately signed.

How did President Bush forge this unity of purpose in a time of division? The answer was simple: Both sides saw a clear goal.

At the time of the president's speech to Congress, the U.S. economy was in bad shape. While economic growth slowed, unemployment rose. In the face of this economic stagnation, members of both parties recognized that we needed an investment recovery to generate greater job creation. That's why they were open to the president's tax reforms.

As the chairman of the President's Council of Economic Advisers, I saw the tax reform negotiations firsthand. I watched a proposal that ordinarily would have been a purely Republican priority become an opportunity for collaboration. To win bipartisan support, President Bush included elements in the tax plan that appealed to Democrats. Likewise, congressional Democrats were willing to consider the president's plan because they saw that it would help move the country toward a long-term goal: higher investment and higher employment.

Contrast that sense of shared purpose to today's world, where some politicians say, "Let's just raise taxes," or, "Let's just cut these programs." Politicians make these kinds of big policy proposals all the time, but they rarely answer the most obvious and important question of all: Toward what end?

There's a reason the most successful CEOs articulate where they want to take a company before they say how they'll get there. If everyone involved agrees on a goal, then they have a way to measure their success. When presented with two paths, people can clearly compare one idea to another. But without a destination at the end of those paths, each person is free to retreat to absolutist positions—and there's no way to truly measure which will lead to greater success.

Solving our nation's challenges isn't a technical problem, as many in the media seem to believe. They think we need an expert to come in and do X or Y. But in most cases, the problem isn't technical—it's political. We don't have leaders who are forced to articulate their objectives and describe how they'd get there.

That's what needs to change. We need our leaders to stop moving from fight to fight—and to start telling us where they want to go. We need leaders who will be honest about the trade-offs involved and the obstacles ahead. And we need leaders with vision, who can map out a better future for our country—and then take the steps we need to get there together.

NO LABELS VOICES
DR. ALICE RIVLIN
Former OMB Director and Vice Chairman
of the Federal Reserve

Today in Washington, DC most people think of the words "bipartisan solution" the way they think of the tooth fairy. It's a nice idea—until you grow up and realize it's a fantasy. But I've seen that fantasy become a reality many times, including twice in the last few years.

Since 2010, I've served on two major bipartisan commissions on the budget, one of which I co-chaired. The first was the Domenici-Rivlin Debt Reduction Task Force, and the second was the Simpson-Bowles Commission. In both cases, the members of these commissions started by agreeing on a common goal: reducing the size of the U.S. debt to below sixty percent of GDP. Once we'd agreed on that objective, it gave us a framework for discussing how to get there.

In the Domenici-Rivlin task force, we had another stipulation as well. We didn't just agree that we wanted to reduce the rate of debt growth. We also agreed that we wouldn't immediately rule out *any* means of getting there.

These two conditions enabled the task force members to work through the problem systematically—looking at all the options. First, we focused on slowing the growth of entitlements. Then we looked at slowing the growth of discretionary spending. But even once we'd agreed on some quite drastic recommendations on those points, the whole group—Republicans and Democrats alike—realized that we couldn't get there without some revenue increases as well.

At that point, we turned to tax reform. And once we looked at our options, we realized we could actually devise a simpler, more progressive tax structure. It would raise more revenue with lower rates, while being friendlier to economic growth. So we added this tax reform piece to the final plan we proposed.

If we had proposed this idea at the beginning, it almost

certainly would have been viewed as a nonstarter. But we were ultimately able to agree on this major decision in the end largely because we had established a shared objective up front.

Domenici-Rivlin achieved unanimity, while Simpson-Bowles only achieved a majority. But both of these commissions demonstrated that a group of people from different political parties could reach major agreement on contentious issues. Today, both parties need to learn the same lesson. In fact, our Constitution gives them no other choice. Our government is set up to force collaboration and dialogue. Even if all the branches of government were controlled by one party, we would *still* need the House, the Senate, and the executive branch to find ways to work together.

Short of amending the Constitution to create a parliamentary system—which is not going to happen—we must break the gridlock by restoring dialogue and cooperation right now. That's the only way we can solve public problems and achieve big goals. It's going to take leadership from Congress and the White House—and we need that leadership now more than ever.

NO LABELS VOICES
DAVE WALKER
Former United States Comptroller General Founder and CEO of the Comeback America Initiative

Management 101 says that if you want to maximize success, mitigate risk, and ensure sustainability for a better future, you need to have three things: a plan, a budget, and a set of desired outcomes or goals. The United States has been a republic since 1789 and we have none of those. We're zero for three. That's a strikeout. It's no wonder we have so many problems and ongoing political controversies.

It's important to rally the nation around a set of principles and values that can bring people together rather than divide them. And it's equally important to determine a set of common goals for the greater good. By working together across party lines and bridging ideological divides, it's possible to agree on a set of principles, values, and goals that can break the gridlock in Washington and help pave the way for a better future. This has to happen—and I have demonstrated that it can.

In 2012, I traveled around the country to twenty-seven states. I conducted various town hall meetings, and went to many college campuses and gatherings of business and community leaders to talk about the country's fiscal challenges. After discussing the gravity of our financial situation to a gathering of voters in two special town hall meetings, ninety-seven percent of the group agreed that putting our finances in order should be a top priority for the president and the Congress. Then we got around ninety-two percent agreement on a set of principles and values to accomplish that objective.

Next, we offered a range of paths forward to achieve that goal, such as tax, Social Security, Medicare and Medicaid, health care, defense, management, and political reforms. We got anywhere from seventy-seven to ninety percent agreement on the proposed reforms. You can't get much better than that.

When I became U.S. comptroller general in 1998 and head of the GAO (then called the General Accounting Office), the agency, in existence since 1921, had never had a strategic plan. In order to "lead by example," we began to develop one, and in January 2000 rolled it out. It's the closest thing the U.S. government has to a comprehensive and government-wide strategic plan. We used that plan to reorganize and reform the agency (including changing the agency's name to the Government Accountability Office). Eight years later, we had a thirteen percent smaller staff, were fifty percent more productive, had three times the outcome-based results, and were generating a $110 return on every dollar invested in the agency.

It's pretty basic. If you don't have a plan, you're flying blind. Right now, the federal government is flying blind in a mountain of debt with huge unfunded obligations that threaten our future position in the world, our future standard of living, our future national security, and even our future domestic tranquility. And our fiscal challenge is only one of many challenges we face.

Washington is badly broken. We have a high degree of hyperpartisanship and a great ideological divide. It's important that we take steps to look longer and broader and to focus on common goals and desired outcomes in order to bring people together rather than divide them apart. Once both sides agree on a set of shared objectives, Congress should use these goals to inform new legislation and to guide its reauthorization, appropriations, and oversight responsibilities. It's critically important that we have a strategic plan if we're ever going to break the gridlock. The time to act is now!

FROM SINGAPORE TO INDIA TO CHINA: STRATEGY IN ACTION

BY GOVERNOR JON HUNTSMAN

I don't just believe in these principles in the abstract. I've seen them in my own life. So now I'd like to offer my own chapter – a story about how shared visions and common goals have helped make some of my biggest achievements possible—even when they seemed impossible at first.

During my career, I've lived overseas four times and traveled to countless foreign countries. From Singapore to Brazil to the United Kingdom, they've been very different places. But most of them have had one very important thing in common: They've had national strategies. As countries, they've had clear ideas about where they need to go, and how they want to get there. Today, they are taking clear steps to strengthen their economies and their nations as a whole.

Right now, the United States is competing with these nations. But instead of pursuing clear goals to strengthen our future, our government can barely keep the lights on right now. We've fallen behind domestically, and we've tarnished our image internationally. We're moving from political crisis to political showdown with no end in sight and no plans for our future prosperity.

It doesn't have to be this way. When I ran for governor of Utah, my first shot at public office, I did what any sensible American would do: I drew up a plan. A plan that was short on politics and long on solutions.

Right away, I brought together experts and stakeholders from across our state. Citizens, small business leaders, academics, and a whole lot of other people offered ideas. In the end, we put together a ten-point plan for Utah, and I made clear that if I were elected, that was the strategy I was going to pursue.

The idea behind that ten-point plan was simple: We needed to make our economy stronger and more competitive. We saw that there were practical steps that could get us to those goals—not because one party said so, but because they were the right ideas for our state.

I was lucky enough to win that election. So once I got to the governor's office, the work began. I started consulting with members of both parties, making the case for why this plan was right for our state. I told them why I thought it would help us get ahead. And eventually, enough Democrats and Republicans got behind this shared agenda for our state. By the time I left office, we had implemented every single one of our ten original goals.

You might think that the only way to reach any kind of bipartisan agreement was to settle on watered-down, small-bore proposals. But the truth is, many of these were ambitious undertakings. We fundamentally reformed Utah's tax code to essentially implement a flat tax. We improved primary education and the colleges in our state. We worked to build our state's infrastructure so that it lived up to the promise of the twenty-first century.

By the time we were done, the results were clear. We had the lowest unemployment and the highest rates of economic growth in the nation. Our state's economy was growing the fastest in the nation. According to the Pew Foundation, we were also the best-managed state in the nation. Everybody in Utah felt uplifted by this bipartisan success.

This was one of those increasingly rare instances in politics where we were able to put the will of the people at the forefront of politics. And it was only possible because we brought both parties together around a shared vision reflecting the collective interests of the state.

We did it in Utah—and we can do it as a country. Today

our leaders need to stop focusing on narrow interests and start putting the will of the American people before politics.

The American people don't want political dysfunction. They want us to solve the biggest problems facing our country today. That's why I firmly believe that we need a national strategy for economic competitiveness—something that will keep us focused on the next generation and not the next election cycle. Something that allows us to put country first, well before the interests of political parties. I'm delighted that this book will offer the first steps toward that goal.

VISION SHARED: A COMMON AGENDA IN WEST VIRGINIA

BY SENATOR JOE MANCHIN

I grew up in the small coal-mining town of Farmington, West Virginia, the kind of town where it was just natural for people to look out for each other. I learned a lot growing up in that special little town—about community, compassion, and courage. I also learned a lot working after school and weekends at my grandfather's grocery store. In fact, that's where I learned one of the most important lessons of my life—one that has guided me every day of my life. "If you want to help people," Papa Joe used to tell me, "you've got to keep yourself strong, and not just physically and mentally, but financially strong as well."

Fifty years later, as I stood on the steps of the West Virginia State Capitol with one hand on the Bible and the other raised to the heavens, being sworn in as the Mountain State's thirty-fourth governor, I thought about so many things that had brought me to that special moment in my life. But more than anything, I kept hearing the words of my grandfather. And I thought to myself, "If I'm going to help West Virginians to the best of my ability, not only do I have to keep myself strong—I've got to make sure our state is financially strong."

From the very start of my governorship, that was my mission—to make sure West Virginia had a solid financial foundation. And I sought advice everywhere on how to make sure we fixed any cracks in that foundation. I went to New York to talk to the financial experts on Wall Street, asking them what they thought about my little state, and they were honest. Our Achilles' heel was our workers' compensation system. It was so broken and so expensive, Wall Street said, that nobody wanted to invest in West Virginia. And that meant new jobs and economic expansion were out of the question.

Then fixing our state's workers' compensation system would have to be the place for me to start. Critics said I was biting off more than I could chew. But I had an ace in the hole that put the odds of success in my favor—a diverse group of West Virginians not only committed to improving our state but willing to set aside their personal and political differences to find common ground and commonsense solutions. They called themselves Vision Shared because they shared a vision of a better West Virginia.

Vision Shared had come together years before I was elected governor. It grew out of years of political infighting that had slowed progress in West Virginia—conflicts pitting business against labor, trial lawyers against doctors and hospitals, the same kind of disputes that you can find anywhere in the country.

It hadn't been long since I had lost my first campaign for governor, but I still wanted to make a difference for my state. To me, politics wasn't a career opportunity. It was an opportunity to fix problems. So I joined with some other business leaders, and we sat down with our new governor, Cecil Underwood, to find a better way forward without all the political squabbling. We brought in a development expert. Then the head of the AFL-CIO and other labor organizations joined us. Then the Chamber of Commerce and other representatives of the business community got involved. Then AARP, hospital representatives, doctors, teachers, school groups all came to the table. Before we knew it, virtually every group in the state was represented.

Then came the real breakthrough—we started talking to each other instead of past each other, and we recognized right away how much we had in common. We shared so many goals for West Virginia—encouraging entrepreneurship, improving education, developing our workforce, and promoting research and commercialization. Eventually, the group became an advisory board for our elected officials. It was called Vision Shared—and it is on the front lines promoting West Virginia today.

When I became governor in 2005, I used Vision Shared as my sounding board every time I was trying to get Democrats and Republicans to work together. I could go to the Vision Shared Board and say, "We've all identified the same problems and the same goals. Now together, let's figure out how we get there from here." I could take that consensus back to the politicians, and we would be well on our way toward solutions—even for problems that once seemed unsolvable, like our broken workers' compensation system.

In that case, we got all the stakeholders in one room. Every group had different priorities, but eventually we were able to convince them of one overriding fact—the current system could not be sustained. That common ground led to higher ground—we replaced an inefficient state-run bureaucracy with a privately run system. And today, it is one of the most successful in the country.

Fixing our workers' compensation system restored confidence in our state government, and we began to see the benefits. Even during the recent recession, we were one of the few states whose credit rating improved on Wall Street. We even had surplus money in the middle of the economic crisis, and we built up a rainy day fund on top of that.

Papa Joe would have been proud.

All of this was possible because people agreed on a shared vision, figuring out how to get there, and then making it a reality, together.

It worked in West Virginia. It can work in Washington. That is why I am so excited about No Labels. It gives us a forum to sit down and work together in Washington, just like Vision Shared did for the Mountain State.

No Labels gives me hope that Washington can actually get back to the business of solving our country's problems together. No Labels gives me hope that Washington can set aside party politics and do what's best for our nation. And that, ultimately, is what keeps America strong.

NO LABELS VOICES
REP. CHRIS GIBSON (R-NY)

I've seen how common goals can bring about success and trust in the most challenging circumstances. In the summer of 2005, I was a battalion commander leading paratroopers in the northern Iraqi city of Tal Afar. It was a very challenging situation with much strife and significant violence and loss of life. There were near-daily gunfights and potential improvised explosive devices around every corner. And all this was going on in a place where temperatures rose on some days to 120 degrees.

My airborne infantry battalion was attached to the 3rd Armored Cavalry Regiment, and our mission was to help the folks there forge a better way of life. We were trying to help the Iraqis restore security, rebuild infrastructure, and get their essential services up and running.

I met with leaders of the various tribes and listened to all their concerns. At times, these tribes were all fighting each other and, in some cases, fighting our troops. The violence and hard feelings were getting in the way of the trust and teamwork that was necessary to do the rebuilding. I said to the sheikhs, "Why don't we focus on an area that everyone could benefit from?" That issue was water. The infrastructure had been badly damaged and the flow of water was impeded.

With the common goal of increasing the access to clean water, for a period of time, the Iraqis set aside their differences and worked together, and we were able to get the water system back up and running. That set the stage for further progress. By focusing on something that we knew needed to get done— the simple task of getting the water to flow—we began the process of forging trust. What we noticed over time was that by improving these sorts of services, the locals, day by day, gained more trust in each other and in their own institutions.

If that sort of teamwork is possible in a combat zone, surely we can get together and focus on common goals here in a land where we have so much more in common than we ever have apart. There will be lots more to talk about. We're going to have to have significant debate before we finally arrive at any consensus. But if we put down achievable goals and then focus our debate on how to accomplish those goals, we will unite our country and move forward together.

NO LABELS VOICES
REP. CHERI BUSTOS (D-IL)

I was a newspaper reporter and editor for seventeen years and then worked for a health system before coming to Congress in 2013. In the private sector, you work with people every day you don't always agree with. Conflicts are daily occurrences, whether it's a heated debate between editors over which story should go on the front page of the newspaper or a struggle over a budget. But I'd still be a rookie-level reporter if I didn't understand how to work together, how to deliver, and how to talk through disagreements.

When I was director of communications at Trinity Regional Health System in Illinois, I didn't always agree with budget decisions coming down from my bosses. In one instance, I was told I had to cut my department budget by one-third. That's a pretty big cut, and it was hard to take.

We came at it from different angles: My chief financial officer was looking out for money. I was looking out for the end product and making sure we could still convey the message we needed to convey. But we both had the same goal—the best interest of the health system. We both knew there had to be some budget constraints, but that my department still had to provide information to the public in meaningful and understandable ways.

So we talked it through. I showed him what would be hurt with a one-third cut. And in the end, we compromised. My department still had to make substantial cuts, but not as dramatic. Though the bosses and I had not started out on the same page, we all felt good about the end result.

We all bring these life experiences with us to Congress. I've learned you can't succeed if you don't understand working together. So right after I was elected in November 2012, I reached out to every other freshman member—thirty-five Republicans and forty-nine other Democrats—either calling them or sitting down for a talk. I would introduce myself and say, "Hey, I look forward to working with you." We had great conversations, talking about family or sports. I talked with Rep. Ted Yoho about pets—he's a veterinarian and I'm a dog lover. Though we operate on different ends of the political spectrum, he's someone I'd like to work with to see if there's at least a starting point on policy.

In all the calls I made, I never once hung up the phone and thought, "I'll never be able to work with that person!"

NO LABELS VOICES
REP. MIKE FITZPATRICK (R-PA)

The concept of trying to find common solutions really sums up my management style, in my private life as an attorney, in my public life as a member of Congress and, before that, a county commissioner.

Before I entered Congress in 2005, I spent ten years as a county commissioner in Bucks County, the quintessential swing district. There are three commissioners on the board and they're never all from the same party. There has to be a minority member. It functions exceedingly well as long as you have people in those roles who want to work together.

Though we only needed two votes to pass a resolution, my goal during the five years I was chairman was always to get all three. Whenever the Democrat on the board opposed something, I'd say, "What is it you're concerned about, and how can we change this to earn your support?" I couldn't always get there, but I always tried. I felt that was my obligation to the people as well as to myself. In the end, if you have consensus, the result for the people will be better and implementation will be easier. And about ninety-eight percent of the time, we were able to achieve a unanimous decision.

What helped us reach consensus was that the first thing we did after I was appointed to the board in 1995 was come together in a room and set very clear goals. We wanted to tell the people where we were going as a county government, what was important to us, and how we intended to achieve those goals. Then we formed bipartisan task forces to deal with each of the major objectives. Because these goals had been developed in a collaborative way, we knew they were rooted in the best interests of the county. As a result, we had many achievements, including the first ever enterprise zone in Bucks County, which led to thousands of private sector jobs, a voter referendum that resulted in the preservation of ten thousand acres of farmland and parkland, and the first ever human relations council in the county.

Reaching a consensus on goals is more difficult than the implementation of the ideas. It takes leaders who recognize that agreeing to eighty percent of something is better than one hundred percent of nothing. At the county level, the process of trying to get to consensus made all of us better elected officials and better representatives of a diverse community. Of the ten budgets we passed during my ten years as a commissioner, nine were unanimous budgets. I always look back on that tenth budget and think, "Did I try hard enough? Was there something else I could have done?" Washington needs more of that kind of thinking—and that kind of collaboration and agreement on goals.

NO LABELS VOICES
STEPHEN HEINTZ
President of Rockefeller Brothers Fund

It was during an "involuntary sabbatical" in 2012 that I decided to focus my attention on the current state of our democracy.

In the early phase of my career, I'd spent fifteen years in

politics and government in Connecticut and had become a bit jaded. Even in the 1970s and '80s, it was already apparent that money was far too prevalent and influential, and that politics was more of a competitive sport than an effort to get things done. After the Berlin Wall fell, I moved to Eastern Europe and worked to help strengthen the transitions to democracy across the region. Being there for the first decade after the collapse of communism was very exciting and inspiring, and when I returned to America, I was ready to work to revitalize our own democracy.

When I joined the Rockefeller Brothers Fund in 2001, we created a grant-making program to do just that—try to help strengthen and revitalize American democracy. Then in 2012, I had one of those moments that really wakes you up when I was diagnosed with a rare form of leukemia. I spent a year getting chemotherapy and then had a successful bone marrow transplant. Between hospitalization and my time recuperating at home, I was out of work for about nine months.

After I was diagnosed, I made the decision to try to be very disciplined and use the time to study and think about the state of our democracy. I read current literature, historical literature, books, journals, and articles, many of which described the decline in our political culture, the tearing at our social fabric, the growth of economic inequality and decline in economic opportunity.

It was striking to me that a lot of the literature pointed to the same thirty-year period starting in the late 1970s when we went off track, in part because of globalization, advances in technology, and radical changes in the economy, but also, in part, by design—by political decisions and changes in public policy. The more I read, the angrier I got. I concluded that we are adrift as a country and we don't share a sense of national purpose.

We have had this common purpose at moments of great crisis in our history including the country's founding. The Declaration of Independence is an elegant statement of national purpose. There have been other such moments: the Civil War, the fight against fascism, the Cold War, the mission to put a man on the moon, our coming to terms and coming together around civil rights and gender rights. These were moments where the nation struggled but ultimately came together and found a sense of shared national purpose.

We have to come together and once again be the America of our collective dream. It's going to require a strategic agenda for the country based on big national goals that we need to accomplish in this century. And then it's going to take a plan for reforming the political process so we can accomplish those goals, so we can have a truly functioning democratic system.

One of the books I read during my "sabbatical" was a volume commissioned by Nelson Rockefeller in the mid-1950s, when he was chairman of the board here at the RBF and aspired to be president of the United States. He realized he needed a platform of ideas and a brain trust to help him develop the substantive ideas for a presidential campaign. He brought together leaders from business, academia, philanthropy, the non-profit sector, the faith community, and trade unions, and hired staff that included a young Henry Kissinger from Harvard. They spent four years working in sub-panels—on topics ranging from arts and culture to national security—and issued a series of papers with national goals and very specific proposals for each topic that became a book, *Prospect for America*, published in 1961.

Although Nelson obviously didn't get to be president of the United States, John F. Kennedy and later Lyndon B. Johnson used some of the material, and a number of the ideas became national policy.

We have to engage in a similar process of analysis and goal setting today, one that's not just limited to a blue-ribbon commission, but that includes the grassroots engagement of hundreds of thousands if not millions of Americans. It will take a major national conversation over the next couple years—a very serious dialogue about the kinds of goals we want to achieve, the kind of country we want to be, and the kinds of reforms that are necessary to accomplish those purposes.

LEARNING FROM BUSINESS: A RECIPE FOR NATIONAL SUCCESS

BY RON SHAICH
FOUNDER AND CEO OF PANERA BREAD

For a businessman like Ron Shaich, strategic thinking comes naturally. That's why he's been able to found two of the most successful restaurant concepts in America: Au Bon Pain and Panera Bread. No matter what, Ron has always had a clear sense of where his business needs to go. That's why he's been so successful. And he strongly believes that the United States needs to catch up with this kind of thinking.

—Jon

As a CEO, my most important imperative is figuring out what actions we have to take today to get us to where we want to be tomorrow. In every meeting, regardless of topic, the most important questions have always been the same. What are we trying to achieve? What are our criteria for success? And what do we need to do to make sure we accomplish our goals?

This was what we discussed in our very first conversations relative to starting Panera Bread. At the time, the restaurant world was essentially split between fine dining and fast food. And within the world of fast food, most operators sought to deliver mass-produced, lower-quality fare at very low prices.

We looked at that and realized a significant number of people wanted something better. They wanted food they could respect served by people with self-respect. They wanted it served in an environment that engaged them. They were willing to pay a bit more, but they also wanted something different—something more—coming back across the counter.

From that moment on, our strategy was clear. We decided to fill in that niche and offer that something more. Once we'd made that overarching decision, every other action we took—from developing the items on our menu to creating the layout of our restaurants—was designed to bring that goal into reality. It was all about building a differentiated alternative for the guest. And in the decades since, we've stayed true to that central, guiding plan.

There were times when we were tested, but we never wavered from that fundamental strategy. When the recession hit, many restaurants started cutting back on costs. We were under a great deal of pressure to do that, too. But we knew cutting costs would mean longer lines, dirtier restaurants, and lower-quality food. In short, it would go against our fundamental strategy of delivering something more.

So at the height of the recession, instead of pulling back, we decided to invest, consistent with our strategy. Indeed, we chose to improve the quality of the experience because we still believed that was what mattered. As a result we started rolling out new, innovative menu items and invested in extra labor in our cafes. We also chose to increase our growth rate by fifty percent to take advantage of the opportunities for high-quality investment that the recession provided.

In the end, we saw our profits skyrocket during the depths of the recession, and our stock followed course, roughly doubling in size during the same period (January 2008 to mid-2009), which set the stage for even more impressive growth in the years that followed. And that was possible only because we looked beyond the short-term pressures of the moment, and kept our eyes trained on the plan that really mattered.

When I look at Congress right now, I see them making the exact opposite choice. Our leaders aren't thinking about how we're going to compete in the long term. They're almost entirely focused on getting through the next election or the next legislative session. But if one focuses only on the immediate future, I can promise an outcome similar to that shared by many of my competitors—the ones who optimized their short-term profitability and provided Panera the opportunity to leap ahead of them.

Ultimately, I would argue that if you're a leader, you have a responsibility not only to survive, but to lead. And if you are an elected official, you have a responsibility to leave this country better than you found it. That's why I believe our leaders in Washington need to look beyond the issue of the week. They need to stop focusing on keeping score and political games. Instead, they need to finally agree on a shared strategy for our country. Ultimately, that's how we'll regain our competitive advantage as a nation, and that's how we will continue to succeed.

NO LABELS VOICES
KATHERINE M. GEHL
President and CEO, Gehl Foods, Inc.

In business, we would have tremendous problems if we didn't have a strategy everyone understood and was invested in. We run a manufacturing company in the heartland, and like many manufacturing companies, we are going through a major transition from a traditional, command-and-control facility to the kind of world-class facility you need to be competitive in today's global economy.

That means more empowerment and opportunity for the employees, but also more accountability. It's a very different way of working for the three hundred people at my company, and change is hard. There are trade-offs. People like doing things the way they're used to doing them. If the employees didn't have a shared understanding of our future vision, we would spend all our time on the negative aspects of the changes. Instead, a clearly communicated strategy can bring people aboard and enroll them in making the effort and taking action to reach the goal. A shared vision and strategy creates possibility both for the company and for employees as individuals.

I think the biggest promise for a national strategy lies in the opportunity it provides not only for enrolling leaders of both political parties, but even more importantly, for enrolling the citizens who have to support the direction and the difficult choices required—because change isn't easy.

It's essential to note, however, that we don't just have a strategy problem in this country. We have an execution problem. That's because the political parties, which are private organizations, exercise vast control over the process of both elections and governing. In addition to a strategic plan, we need to keep pressing for the reforms that No Labels has called for to help make Congress, the presidency, and government work better and to get beyond partisan roadblocks.

It all ties together. If we don't change the way we do business, then our ability to execute our strategy and achieve our goals will be hampered. We need the initiatives that form the foundation of No Labels along with a national strategic agenda. That's a winning combination!

NO LABELS VOICES
ANDREW TISCH
Co-Chairman of the Board and Chairman of
the Executive Committee, Loews Corporation

Throughout my business career, I've found that the first step toward success is clarity of mission. If a mission is clear, it stands the greatest chance of being achieved and the greatest chance of rallying people together with unanimity of purpose.

That clarity of mission is what's missing in Washington today. There is no unanimity of vision. Instead, you've got two completely different groups that are battling for the hearts and minds of the public. Everyone is arguing about strategy, but there's no clarity on what the ultimate goal is. For our country to move forward, we need a very strong national agenda based on consensus and a clear set of goals.

I've seen the power of having a shared sense of mission. Several years ago, then-New York Mayor Mike Bloomberg proposed the idea of a contest among universities to build a new computer sciences and high-tech campus on Manhattan's Roosevelt Island. The whole concept seemed to be written so that Stanford University would win the contract. A lot of people at Cornell University, where I'm on the board of trustees, said, "Hey! This may be something that's good for Cornell as well as the community and plays to our core strengths." So without a tremendous amount of communication or coordination, a number of different groups at Cornell proceeded down the same path.

The mission was so strong in everyone's mind that there was absolutely no choreography necessary in order to get to where we had to be. Students, faculty, alumni, friends ... everybody knew exactly what the mission was and was pulling in unison. One group was writing up the proposal. I used my political connections to make sure our voice was heard in city hall. Somebody else with strong connections to labor was off organizing labor groups and unions. Another group started an alumni petition. Everybody was working towards the same goal, and ultimately Stanford was outflanked. We won in a head-to-head competition, and will soon be breaking ground for the $2 billion campus.

When a company is in real trouble, you often see this kind of cohesive effort in turnaround management. A great CEO rallies the troops by letting everybody know exactly what the issues are and what success will look like and, importantly, how to get there. It's what we did when Loews took over Bulova in 1979. We turned around a small bankrupt watchmaker and made it a successful company by agreeing on what constituted success and then coming up with a plan to achieve that success. It took us five years to go from steep decline to the breakeven point, and then another couple of years to get to profitability.

Business tends to be more a dictatorship than a democracy. In the end, the CEO makes the decisions and faces the greatest consequences. But most great CEOs try to do things collaboratively. It's time our political leaders apply a bit of turnaround management, form a consensus, and articulate a clear vision for this country. We have seen that happen after D-Day, in parts of the Kennedy and Reagan administrations, and even after 9-11 for a while. And it's possible once again today—especially with the strong advocacy of a group like No Labels.

There's a quote I'm fond of that underscores the challenge we face today. The author is unknown, but the truth behind the words is unmistakable:

> "A democracy is always temporary in nature; it simply cannot exist as a permanent form of government. A democracy will continue to exist up until the time that voters discover that they can vote themselves generous gifts from the public treasury. From that moment on, the majority always votes for the candidates who promise the most benefits from the public treasury, with the result that every democracy will finally collapse due to loose fiscal policy, which is always followed by a dictatorship.
>
> "The average age of the world's greatest civilizations from the beginning of history has been about 200 years. During those 200 years, these nations always progressed through the following sequence: From bondage to spiritual faith; From spiritual faith to great courage; From courage to liberty; From liberty to abundance; From abundance to selfishness; From selfishness to complacency; From complacency to apathy; From apathy to dependence; From dependence back into bondage."

We don't have to go this route. We can still come together to make our nation stronger. I think there's a critical mass at the center of our electorate—I call it the middle eighty percent—that will come together around a national agenda. And that's what it will take to move our country forward.

AMERICA'S LEADERSHIP CHECKLIST

BY PROFESSOR MICHAEL USEEM
THE WHARTON SCHOOL

Michael Useem is a longtime scholar of leadership. He's studied great leaders and leaders who have fallen short—and he knows what it takes for a nation to succeed. Today Useem is a professor at the University of Pennsylvania's prestigious Wharton business school, and from that position he has continued to observe our country's elected leaders closely. In this chapter, he argues that it will take strong leadership to build consensus around shared goals and a common vision for our country. He elaborates on the kind of leadership we need today—and the kind of leaders we should look for—and vote for—in elections to come.

—Jon

For the ideas in this volume to come to life, everybody's leadership will be vital. Otherwise, even the best ideas will never make it off the page.

Right now, however, many of our national leaders appear to be paralyzed, unable or unwilling to rise above the gridlock. They act as if they are hopelessly trapped by the political congestion we have all come to know too well.

It's understandable that many politicians might consider even the smallest, most commonsense initiatives to be futile in the face of Washington's gridlock. Why would any elected official pursue fresh thinking or big ideas when interest groups always seem ready to stand in the way and political landmines are always ready to explode?

In many ways this sense of resignation is understandable.

After all, the logjam on Capitol Hill is certainly among the worst of recent memory. For many in Washington, inaction at the moment seems the only feasible action.

But of course our history has been punctuated by moments far worse, and leaders during the hardest times have confronted far more intractable conflicts. Abraham Lincoln faced a breakaway republic, Franklin Delano Roosevelt a world at war, and Nelson Mandela a ruthless regime. Yet each found a way forward where others saw none. They persisted, and they prevailed.

Our discords today are not as profound, and the stakes not as momentous, but our differences certainly do run very deep. And resolution of those differences—or our failure to resolve them—will undoubtedly define our country's direction for many years to come.

We know from experience that a nation's leadership has the greatest impact when a country is facing its greatest uncertainties, when the contentious issues are especially nettlesome, and when the most fateful decisions are particularly complex. It's thus times like these when a nation's leadership is most important— and when we need our leaders to reach for something greater than the pettiness of the moment.

In other words, we need *more* national leadership now, precisely because this is one of those very moments when exercising that leadership has become all the more impactful— and all the more difficult.

What will it take for our national leadership to break out of that deadlock? I've been studying leadership for quite some time, and I've found that the answer really requires no rocket science. In fact, the way forward for our leaders can be distilled down to just a half a dozen plain old-fashioned leadership ingredients. This is what we will all want to see more of among those most responsible for the future of the country:

1. *Take charge:* Embrace action. If you are positioned to make a difference, no matter how modest, take responsibility.
2. *Define a vision and a strategy:* Formulate a clear and powerful view of the solutions we want and a way of getting there.

3. *Communicate persuasively:* Characterize that vision and that strategy in ways people cannot forget.

4. *Embrace the front lines:* Stay close to those most directly engaged with the work of the initiative, drawing the best from each.

5. *Build leadership throughout the ranks:* Develop a capacity for all of us to help take charge, each in our own way.

6. *Place public interest first:* In communicating a vision, setting the strategy, and taking actions, common purpose always comes first, political self-interest last.

We have witnessed all of these qualities powerfully at work when Abraham Lincoln mobilized his "team of rivals" to save the Union, when Ronald Reagan and Tip O'Neill garnered budgets without brinksmanship, and even in everyday life when citizens get on with the business of getting things done.

These ideas might sound obvious, but they've been shockingly absent from our political discourse over the last several years. Instead of embracing the precepts to resolve real problems, too many of our elected officials have devolved into political gamesmanship. But if our leaders can embrace just a handful of very simple principles, we believe that a transformative moment lies ahead.

Governor Jon Huntsman, Senator Joe Manchin, and some eighty members of Congress have already embraced these principles in building the problem-solving foundation that defines No Labels. And in doing so, they've already begun to change how Washington works.

Their active leadership—and our active leadership—has become essential for moving the No Labels ideas into reality. Together, our combined leadership can advance a genuine national strategy for a country that otherwise seems stuck in neutral or worse.

NO LABELS VOICES
THOMAS F. "MACK" MCLARTY
White House Chief of Staff for President Bill Clinton (D)

One of my most enduring memories of my time as President Bill Clinton's White House chief of staff was sitting in the Roosevelt Room with Newt Gingrich and George Stephanopoulos. They weren't debating a policy dispute or hammering out a contentious bargain. They were counting votes, together.

It was November 17, 1993, and the House of Representatives was voting on the North American Free Trade Agreement (NAFTA)—an effort to create a vibrant North American market that reached from the Yukon to the Yucatan.

NAFTA had been negotiated by President George H.W. Bush's administration, but the Clinton administration was determined to see it through. President Clinton understood that in an age of globalization, America's future depended on competing with the rest of the world, not retreating from it.

This was an instance where the president and members of the opposing party not only agreed on a shared goal, but actively worked together to secure it. Indeed, another enduring memory from that time was the Rose Garden event where President Carter, President Bush, and President Clinton stood shoulder to shoulder in calling for NAFTA's passage.

In the end, NAFTA passed both houses of Congress on a strongly bipartisan basis, but with more Republicans than Democrats voting in favor. The president proudly signed the agreement into law. At the time, this was the most comprehensive free trade agreement on earth. In the years since, it's been vital to our nation's economic growth; today, U.S. trade with Canada and Mexico supports fourteen million good U.S. jobs.

The Clinton years may be remembered for periods of partisan discord, but this was just one example of many where the two parties came together. The president and his staff savored any opportunity to work alongside the Republicans in Congress. We all liked it better when we could find common ground and work to achieve a common goal.

That was true with the 1996 Welfare-to-Work initiative that helped move millions of Americans from the welfare rolls to paid employment; the 1997 budget agreement that cut spending, cut the deficit, and set us on course for a balanced budget; and almost all major foreign policy issues. Both parties agreed on where we needed to go, and then we found a way to get there together.

If we had been able to agree on more shared goals, I'm sure the achievements would have been even more numerous. After all, we've also seen this approach work with incredible success at the state level. America's governors have legislatures to deal with, too. But they almost always find a way to work together, even if it means reaching across party lines.

As President Clinton wrote in the *New York Times* on the tenth anniversary of the welfare reform legislation, "This style of cooperative governing is anything but a sign of weakness. It is a measure of strength, deeply rooted in our Constitution and history, and essential to the better future that all Americans deserve, Republicans and Democrats alike."

We need that same spirit in Washington today. We need the leaders of both parties in Washington to find a shared path forward once again. I believe that this is possible—and for the good of our country, I hope it happens soon.

NO LABELS VOICES
JAMES A. BAKER III
White House Chief of Staff for President Ronald Reagan (R) and Former Secretary of State

No one was more of an idealist than President Ronald Reagan. He believed in the noble concepts of American exceptionalism, and he possessed concrete notions about how to maintain it. Keep spending low, income taxes down, and get out of the way of the private sector so that it can be the world's most efficient economic engine.

But The Gipper was also a realist. He understood that Americans judge our presidents on more than their convictions and fanciful rhetoric. Americans also judge them by their accomplishments, by their ability to get things done in Washington—particularly when times get tough.

Few times were tougher than when Reagan was inaugurated in 1981. He faced an economy plagued by the so-called "misery index," with both inflation and unemployment hovering above ten percent. *Newsweek* proclaimed that President Reagan had inherited "the most dangerous economic crisis since Franklin Roosevelt took office forty-eight years ago."

Reagan got to work, and he did what a leader should do. He built consensus around the objectives he wanted to achieve. He worked with the Democratic-controlled Congress toward the shared goal of economic revitalization—and almost immediately, he began to see success.

The president and the Democrats in Congress had real policy disagreements, of course. It wasn't always easy for them to work together. As Reagan's White House chief of staff at the time, I can remember the president and Democratic House Speaker Tip O'Neill yelling at one another during their negotiations in the Oval Office. They would go at it tooth and nail for long stretches. But once their business discussions had concluded, the two would retire for a drink and to tell Irish stories.

Eventually, they struck deals. Before the end of his first year in office, Reagan and the Democratic-controlled Congress passed the Economic Recovery Tax Act of 1981, which, among other things, dropped the top tax rate from seventy percent to fifty percent. They later worked together to reduce the top rate to twenty-eight percent.

Neither side got everything that it wanted in these negotiations. Taxes were lowered, as Reagan desired. But spending was not reduced, as he had hoped. Compromise was not a dirty word. It was a way to get things done.

Some in his party criticized President Reagan for not holding to his principles, for caving in to Democrats. But

I can remember the president repeatedly telling me that he'd rather get eighty percent of what he wanted than go over the cliff with his flag flying. With that approach incorporated into his DNA, Reagan ushered in an era of peace, prosperity, and American conservatism.

The economy responded. By 1984, the misery index had been cut in half from its level when Reagan took office. Reagan's pro-growth policies resulted in ninety-six months of unbroken economic growth starting in 1983, the creation of eighteen million new jobs during that same period, and the eradication of inflation and high interest rates.

Ronald Reagan knew how to fight when he had to. But he also knew when to work with the other side for the good of the country. He was a principled pragmatist. Our leaders in Washington should take a look at that Reagan playbook and take the same approach today.

CONCLUSION
NOVEMBER 8, 2016

BY NO LABELS

Think about what our country could look like with a set of shared goals and a national strategic agenda. Imagine how much better off we would be. Well, thanks to No Labels, we don't have to just imagine anymore. We can start building that stronger country today. The cause is urgent, and now is the time. Let's do this together.

—Jon

It's Tuesday, November 8, 2016. You've just woken up, gotten the kids off to school, and swung by the local community center to cast your vote before work. Today we're electing a new Congress and a new president of the United States.

It's time to ask: When you step out of the voting booth, what kind of country do you want to walk back into?

If we stay on the path we're on now, it's not hard to imagine what that country will look like. A hopelessly divided Washington. A president more devoted to party than to country. An opposition party more concerned with putting up obstacles than coming to the negotiating table. Elected leaders on all sides obsessed with scoring political points—and not many interested in the real challenges facing ordinary Americans.

In other words, it will be just like today. Except all of our problems will have gotten worse. Is that what you want to vote for?

Or do you want to choose a different path? A path that

includes a problem-solving president and a functioning Congress. A path that includes a new governing process where we actually agree on where we need to go as a country—and then collaborate to find a way to get there together.

Imagine what this country could look like. Before the State of the Union, the president and the leader of the opposition meet to talk about their goals for the year. They offer an honest assessment of the progress we've made and where we still need to go. And when the president stands before the country to deliver his or her first State of the Union, both sides of the aisle stand up and applaud.

Imagine what the halls of Congress could look like if members of different parties started meeting regularly to have frank and open discussions about where we need to go as a country. Suddenly, they aren't just trying to score political points or embarrass the other side. They're working to move our country forward. No one in Congress forgets about their deeply held beliefs or the areas where they disagree. But there are plenty of issues where they *can* agree—and when that happens, they don't just allow their different parties to drive them apart.

Instead of government shutdowns and crisis governance, we get a sensible budget every year that's designed to achieve a set of goals we've all agreed on. And before long, we'll be well on the way toward balancing that budget.

Instead of self-inflicted economic wounds, our leaders have come together and told the country that job creation is their top priority. And they didn't just talk about creating jobs—they started taking action. Now jobs are returning home, and all across the country men and women are returning to work and taking home paychecks that can support their families.

We're producing more and more energy at home, and we're using it in more sustainable ways. Within a few years, we won't need to import oil from unfriendly governments just to keep our country up and running. Instead, we've already seen a new energy economy start to blossom here at home. And it's a shift that comes with millions of good American jobs.

When you pass children on the street, you feel confident

that our government will keep its sacred promises to our next generation. Social Security and Medicare are secure—and Americans who have worked all their lives are able to retire with the peace of mind and dignity they deserve.

As these challenges are addressed, our leaders are building momentum to take on even greater problems. For a long time, we've recognized that we need to do more to make sure every child in America has access to a world-class education. We've known that we need to do more to support research, development, and innovation here at home. It's been clear that we need to do better in so many ways—from improving health care to supporting small businesses to strengthening our national security.

All of these issues have plagued our country for years. We've all known it. But now that we've started fixing some of our most foundational problems, we finally have the resources—and the energy—to take the actions we need.

Most important of all, America has leaders who are actually leading once again. They've proven that they can actually still come together around important objectives. They've proven that they can still get things done. And it's clear that this is just the beginning.

This vision doesn't have to be a fantasy. Every one of these items should be common sense for our leaders in Washington. In fact, for a long time we would have thought this was the bare minimum a functioning government would get done. That's not too much to ask again. As a nation, we still have every element for success at our fingertips. America boasts the world's greatest universities, the greatest minds, an innovative potential just waiting to take off. We have men and women in every corner of this country aching to start new businesses and try out new ideas. And we have the rule of law that means they can do it.

Wherever you look in America, you see amazing potential. A manufacturing sector still poised for a renaissance. A natural gas boom that could power our future. The most amazing moment in technological history—with more great ideas percolating wherever you look.

Today our nation is more diverse, more resourceful, and more interconnected than ever before. We have so much working in our favor. We just need the leadership to take advantage of these strengths.

In the end, it all comes down to one last question: Are you happy with the way our government is working right now?

If you're content with how our government is operating, then this movement isn't for you. But if you're part of the vast majority of Americans who desperately want our leaders to start working together once again, then we need you. We need you to join our campaign to change politics in America. We need you to add your voice to our call for shared goals and a national strategic agenda.

Together, we need to call on every member of Congress and every candidate for office to get behind this campaign. Because above all, this campaign's success is going to take real leadership from Washington. We need leaders who will commit to work together, to find common goals, to work to achieve them without constant fighting and division.

We don't expect anyone to shed their identity when they join this movement. No one will ever have to check his or her principles or priorities at the door. And in fact, this diversity makes the movement stronger. It empowers our movement with the energy of every point on the political spectrum. It recognizes that great ideas can come from anywhere. This is a movement that will welcome anyone, so long as they are open to one simple idea: People with different beliefs really can set aside the labels and work to find common ground.

As we mentioned early in this book, ninety-seven percent of Americans told us in a poll last year that it's important for our next president to be a problem solver. *Ninety-seven percent*. Eighty percent told us that we need one set of shared Democratic and Republican goals for our country when the next president takes office. Over the next three years, we're going to be on a campaign to answer that call.

We have to start now—we don't have any time to waste. Some have argued that redistricting or campaign finance reform can solve our troubles. And while these are admirable causes, we don't have the time to wait for them to gain momentum, pass into law, and finally kick into action. It could take decades—and we need a better government today. That means pushing our leaders to be better—to give us the kind of government our nation deserves. And if they won't, then the answer is to elect the leaders who will.

We can't simply accept a status quo where our government doesn't work. We should urgently insist that our best days can still be ahead of us—as long as our leaders actually start leading once again.

This won't be easy. It might take an election or two to get enough of those problem-solving leaders into office. In fact, Washington is so toxic that right now that it might not even be possible until the next presidential administration takes the reins. But we're in this for the long haul. This is going to be a multi-year movement to ensure that the next American president is a problem solver. And just as importantly, it's a campaign to ensure that this new president will have a problem-solving infrastructure waiting for them when they step into office.

If we want this campaign to succeed over the next few years, we're going to need partners like you. The next chance you have, please email **JackMcCullough@NoLabels.org** and tell us your ideas for reaching the goals we've laid out. Go to **NoLabels.org** and sign on to our campaign for a new, shared American vision. We'll keep in touch every step of the way, because we want you to be involved throughout this process. Our goal is to get one million Americans to endorse this idea— because as we've learned again and again, when the American people come together to call for something with one voice, the politicians start to listen. The more people who tell their leaders that we need a common purpose through shared goals, the sooner we can start to turn this ship around.

So please, join our campaign. Tell your leaders that enough is enough. And tell them that next time you walk into the voting booth, you're not going to just rubber stamp the same politics of division and destruction. From now on, you're only going to vote for problem solvers. And if they want your vote, they had better stop fighting and start fixing.

CONNECT WITH NO LABELS

If you believe it's time for our leaders to start coming together around a national strategic agenda, then please get in touch and join our campaign. This is your movement—and we need your help to change politics for good.

SIGN UP TO JOIN THE MOVEMENT AT
WWW.NOLABELS.ORG

 @NOLABELSORG

 WWW.FACEBOOK.COM/NOLABELS

CPSIA information can be obtained at www.ICGtesting.com
Printed in the USA
BVOW01s1834170114

342160BV00010B/106/P